I0496451

STOCK VALUATION HANDBOOK PART 2

Billion Dollar Valuation

BDV Publications

Copyright © 2020 Billion Dollar Valuation

All rights reserved

The characters and events portrayed in this book are fictitious. Any similarity to real persons, living or dead, is coincidental and not intended by the author.

No part of this book may be reproduced, or stored in a retrieval system, or transmitted in any form or by any means, electronic, mechanical, photocopying, recording, or otherwise, without express written permission of the publisher.

Cover design by: BDV Publications
Printed in India

STOCK VALUATION HANDBOOK - PART 2

This is the second DIY Handbook on Discounted Cash flow Valuation of the listed companies in India. Use the values and calculations mentions in this book once you have the excel model downloaded from the link given below.

https://www.eloquens.com/tool/93b3CR0R/billion-dollar-valuation/do-it-yourself-dcf-valuation-blank-template-with-forecasting

The process of valuation is both art and science and hence we leave it up to you for making appropriate assumptions and Formulas. The entire Do-it-yourself valuation takes about 10-15 hours for one company and you can master the process by using this Handbook and our Excel template.

Thorough research is done by our research analysts over a 10 year period on both the qualitative and quantitative factors of these companies. This analysis is then used to forecast financial statements over a period of 5 years.

Hundreds of Annual reports, Investor presentations, Management commentary and Con-call transcripts have been analysed to gather data and analyse the business model and financial conditions. The books do not have any relation with one another and analyses a completely different set of 20 companies each. You can start with any random book from the series and need not begin with the first book.

(Note: All the research done by us is only for educational purposes and should not be seen as Investment recommendations. We are Research analyst and not a SEBI registered Investment Advisor. Our research

completely reflects our personal opinions and not of any of our current or previous employers. Kindly do your own due diligence before Investing)

STRIDES PHARMA VALUATION

Incorporated in 1990, Strides Pharma Science Limited is a global pharmaceutical company headquartered in Bangalore, India. The Company has two business verticals namely Regulated Markets and Emerging Markets. Their core competence is in the development and manufacture of a wide range of niche and technically pharmaceutical products. The company is also amongst the world's largest soft gelatin capsule manufacturers. From here, we go ahead with Strides Pharma Valuation and Intrinsic Value of its shares.

Read more here: **Strides Pharma Shares Fundamental Analysis**
Methodology Used:

Discounted cash flow (DCF) is a valuation method used to estimate the value of an investment based on its expected future cash flows. DCF analysis attempts to figure out the value of an investment today, based on projections of how much money it will generate in the future. The following step by step procedure is followed.

1. Determining the Revenue Growth Rates
2. Forecasting the Financial Statements
3. Deriving the FCFF and FCFE
4. Calculating the Terminal Value
5. Calculating the Discount Rate
6. Discounting the Cashflows

7. Arriving at the Intrinsic Value of the Shares
Step 1: Determining the Revenue Growth Rates

We arrive at the below table by using the past and expected future performance of both the company and the economy. This along with adjustments to changes in the management expectations, extraordinary events and other macro factors give the revenue growth rates for Strides Pharma Valuation.

Financial Year	Revenue Growth Rate
Year 1	-10%
Year 2	22%
Year 3	16%
Year 4	15%
Year 5	20%

Step 2: Forecasting the Financial Statements

The financial statements are forecasted for a period of 5 years using the annual report data of the company. The assumptions used for forecasting are tabulated below. The Excel model is completely editable and can be adjusted for specific changes which may happen over a period of time.

Assumptions Control Sheet	
Income Statement	
Average COGS as Percentage of Revenue	45.00%
Research and Development as Percentage of Revenue	0.00%
Sales, General and administrative as Percentage of Revenue	4.50%
Other operating expenses as Percentage of Revenue	30.00%
Other income (expense) as Percentage of Revenue	0.01%
Balance Sheet	
Short Term Debt as Percentage of Total Assets	16.15%
Long Term Debt as Percentage of Total Assets	23.88%
Cash and Cash Equivalents as Percentage of Revenue	11.13%
Short Term Equivalents as Percentage of Revenue	31.54%
Accounts Receivables as Percentage of Revenue	33.66%
Inventory as Percentage of Revenue	23.49%
Prepaid Expenses as Percentage of Revenue	4.74%
Other Current Assets as Percentage of Revenue	9.09%
Gross property, plant and equipment as Percentage of Revenue	43.70%
Intangible assets as Percentage of Revenue	47.75%
Other long-term assets as Percentage of Revenue	19.60%
Accounts payable as Percentage of Revenue	26.76%
Corporate Tax Rate	22.00%
Other current liabilities as Percentage of Revenue	12.63%
Retained Earnings as as Percentage of Net Income	75.69%
Accumulated other comprehensive income as Percentage of Revenue	40.51%
Cashflow Statement	
Other Working Capital as Percentage of Revenue	5.12%

Step 3: Deriving the FCFF and FCFE

Free cash flow to the firm (FCFF) represents the amount of cash flow from operations available for distribution after accounting for depreciation expenses, taxes, working capital, and investments. FCFF is a measurement of a company's profitability after all expenses and reinvestments. It is given as follows.

Free cash flow to equity (FCFE) is a measure of how much cash is available to the equity shareholders of a company after all expenses, reinvestment, and debt are paid. FCFE is a measure of equity capital usage.

F/S Items (INR Millions)	Mar-20	Mar-21	Mar-22	Mar-23	Mar-24
Free Cash Flow	-788	582	1721	2656	4406

to Firm					
Free Cash Flow to Equity	-4044	3818	5330	6853	12606

Step 4: Calculating the Terminal Value

Terminal value (TV) is the value of a business or project beyond the forecast period when future cash flows can be estimated. It assumes that a business will grow at a set growth rate forever after the forecast period. Terminal value often comprises a large percentage of the total assessed value.

Terminal Value Calculation	Units INR Millions
Free Cash Flow to Firm	4406.10
Growth Rate	6.00%
Cost of Capital	11.26%
Terminal Value	88874.18

Step 5: Calculating the Discount Rate

DCF analysis helps assess the viability of a project or investment by calculating the present value of expected future cash flows using a discount rate. Here we use the Weighted average cost of capital (WACC) to discount the cash flow. The below table from the excel model shows the calculation of WACC for Strides Pharma Valuation.

Cost of Equity Calcuation using CAPM	
Risk Free Rate (5 year G-Sec)	5.18%
Stock Beta (Ref: Reuters)	1.40
Beta Unlevered B/(1+ D(1-t)/E)	0.72
Beta Relevered B*(1+ D(1-t)/E)	1.50
Market Return Rm (Nifty 50 10 Year CAGR)	14.25%
Cost of Equity	**18.83%**

Cost of Debt	
Cost of Debt (Interest Expense/Total Debt)	5.85%

Cost of Capital	
Cost of Equity	18.83%
Weight of Equity in Target Capital Structure	41.62%
Cost of Debt	5.85%
Weight of Debt in Capital Structure	58.38%
WACC	**11.26%**

Step 6: Discounting the Cashflows

The WACC and the Cost of Equity for the company calculated in the above step are then used to discount the FCFF, FCFE and Terminal Value calculated in Step 3 and 4. In our case, we'll only consider the FCFF based Intrinsic price of the shares as it represents the cash flow to all the suppliers of capital and not only to the equity shareholders. Thus we arrive at Present value of future FCFF for Strides Pharma Valuation. (Units are INR Millions)

FCFF Calculation	FV	Discounted
Mar-20	-788.33	-708.58
Mar-21	581.75	470.00
Mar-22	1721.12	1249.83
Mar-23	2656.04	1733.62
Mar-24	4406.10	2584.96
Terminal Value	88874.18	52140.49
Present Value (PV)		57470.33

FCFE Calculation	FV	Discounted
Mar-20	-4043.66	-3402.89
Mar-21	3818.39	2704.13
Mar-22	5329.77	3176.36
Mar-23	6852.82	3436.88
Mar-24	12605.88	5320.38
Terminal Value	88874.18	37509.81
Present Value (PV)		48744.67

Step 7: Arriving at the Intrinsic Value of the Shares

Dividing the PV of the FCFF and Terminal Value (the Value of the entire firm) by the number of outstanding shares we get the per share intrinsic value. We can compare this price with the current market price of the stock to get the Discount or Premium to its intrinsic price.

Strides Pharma Valuation	Units
PV in INR Million	57470
No of Shares Outstanding (In Million)	90
Intrinsic Value	638.56

Current Market Price of Share	814
Current Discount/Premium	27%

Intrinsic Value of the Shares: Strides Pharma Valuation

Strides Pharma Valuation and Intrinsic Share Price = INR 638.56

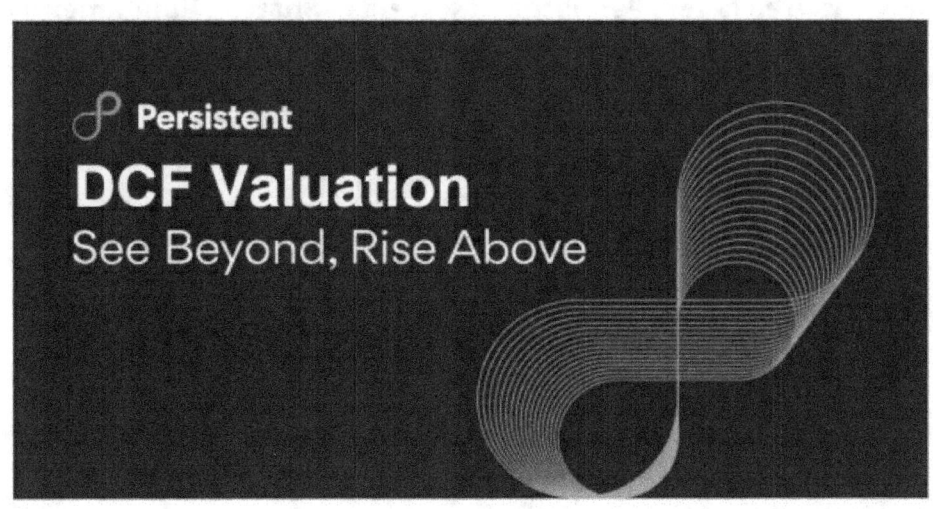

PERSISTENT SYSTEMS VALUATION

Persistent Systems is a global solutions company delivering digital business acceleration and enterprise modernization for businesses across industries and geographies. The company provides technology solutions to Banking, Industrial, Healthcare and Hi-Tech Industry clients across 20+ countries. Persistent has an annual revenue of $ 501 million and has a client base of more than 1000+ across the globe. From here, we go ahead with Persistent Systems Valuation and Intrinsic Value of its shares.

Read more here: Persistent Systems Shares Fundamental Analysis

Methodology Used:

Discounted cash flow (DCF) is a valuation method used to estimate the value of an investment based on its expected future cash flows. DCF analysis attempts to figure out the value of an investment today, based on projections of how much money it will generate in the future. The following step by step procedure is followed.

1. Determining the Revenue Growth Rates
2. Forecasting the Financial Statements
3. Deriving the FCFF and FCFE
4. Calculating the Terminal Value
5. Calculating the Discount Rate
6. Discounting the Cashflows
7. Arriving at the Intrinsic Value of the Shares

Step 1: Determining the Revenue Growth Rates

We arrive at the below table by using the past and expected future performance of both the company and the economy. This along with adjustments to changes in the management expectations, extraordinary events and other macro factors give the revenue growth rates for Persistent Systems Valuation.

Financial Year	Revenue Growth Rate
Year 1	6%
Year 2	17%
Year 3	10%
Year 4	13%
Year 5	14%

Step 2: Forecasting the Financial Statements

The financial statements are forecasted for a period of 5 years using the annual report data of the company. The assumptions used for forecasting are tabulated below. The Excel model is completely editable and can be adjusted for specific changes which may happen over a period of time.

Assumptions Control Sheet	
Income Statement	
Average COGS as Percentage of Revenue	33.50%
Research and Development as Percentage of Revenue	0.00%
Sales, General and administrative as Percentage of Revenue	11.14%
Other operating expenses as Percentage of Revenue	41.00%
Other income (expense) as Percentage of Revenue	2.63%
Balance Sheet	
Short Term Debt as Percentage of Total Assets	0.04%
Long Term Debt as Percentage of Total Assets	0.09%
Cash and Cash Equivalents as Percentage of Revenue	5.06%
Short Term Equivalents as Percentage of Revenue	23.15%
Accounts Receivables as Percentage of Revenue	16.60%
Inventory as Percentage of Revenue	0.00%
Prepaid Expenses as Percentage of Revenue	1.92%
Other Current Assets as Percentage of Revenue	8.99%
Gross property, plant and equipment as Percentage of Revenue	25.83%
Intangible assets as Percentage of Revenue	7.21%
Other long-term assets as Percentage of Revenue	12.67%
Accounts payable as Percentage of Revenue	4.82%
Corporate Tax Rate	22.00%
Other current liabilities as Percentage of Revenue	10.96%
Retained Earnings as as Percentage of Net Income	31.67%
Accumulated other comprehensive income as Percentage of Revenue	37.22%
Cashflow Statement	
Other Working Capital as Percentage of Revenue	1.81%

Step 3: Deriving the FCFF and FCFE

Free cash flow to the firm (FCFF) represents the amount of cash flow from operations available for distribution after accounting for depreciation expenses, taxes, working capital, and investments. FCFF is a measurement of a company's profitability after all expenses and reinvestments. It is given as follows.

Free cash flow to equity (FCFE) is a measure of how much cash is available to the equity shareholders of a company after all expenses, reinvestment, and debt are paid. FCFE is a measure of equity capital usage.

F/S Items (INR Millions)	Mar-20	Mar-21	Mar-22	Mar-23	Mar-24
Free Cash Flow to Firm	3772	5271	5400	6418	7545

| Free Cash Flow to Equity | 3792 | 5423 | 5962 | 7805 | 9413 |

Step 4: Calculating the Terminal Value

Terminal value (TV) is the value of a business or project beyond the forecast period when future cash flows can be estimated. It assumes that a business will grow at a set growth rate forever after the forecast period. Terminal value often comprises a large percentage of the total assessed value.

Terminal Value Calculation	Units INR Millions
Free Cash Flow to Firm	7544.50
Growth Rate	5.50%
Cost of Capital	11.47%
Terminal Value	133384.91

Step 5: Calculating the Discount Rate

DCF analysis helps assess the viability of a project or investment by calculating the present value of expected future cash flows using a discount rate. Here we use the Weighted average cost of capital (WACC) to discount the cash flow. The below table from the excel model shows the calculation of WACC for Persistent Systems Valuation.

Cost of Equity Calcuation using CAPM	
Risk Free Rate (5 year G-Sec)	5.18%
Stock Beta (Ref: Reuters)	0.77
Beta Unlevered B/(1+ D(1-t)/E)	0.77
Beta Relevered B*(1+ D(1-t)/E)	0.77
Market Return Rm (Nifty 50 10 Year CAGR)	14.25%
Cost of Equity	**12.17%**

Cost of Debt	
Cost of Debt (Interest Expense/Total Debt)	7.24%

Cost of Capital	
Cost of Equity	12.17%
Weight of Equity in Target Capital Structure	99.82%
Cost of Debt	7.24%
Weight of Debt in Capital Structure	0.18%
WACC	**12.16%**

Step 6: Discounting the Cashflows

The WACC and the Cost of Equity for the company calculated in the above step are then used to discount the FCFF, FCFE and Terminal Value calculated in Step 3 and 4. In our case, we'll only consider the FCFF based Intrinsic price of the shares as it represents the cash flow to all the suppliers of capital and not only to the equity shareholders. Thus we arrive at Present value of future FCFF for Persistent Systems Valuation. (Units are INR Millions)

STOCK VALUATION HANDBOOK PART 2

FCFF Calculation	FV	Discounted
Mar-20	5569.66	4965.78
Mar-21	3322.95	2641.44
Mar-22	4840.15	3430.32
Mar-23	5034.66	3181.29
Mar-24	5680.32	3200.11
Terminal Value	89968.62	50685.45
Present Value (PV)		68104.39

FCFE Calculation	FV	Discounted
Mar-20	5588.43	4982.11
Mar-21	3326.79	2644.07
Mar-22	4841.77	3430.64
Mar-23	5037.80	3182.26
Mar-24	5684.38	3201.12
Terminal Value	89968.62	50665.23
Present Value (PV)		68105.45

Step 7: Arriving at the Intrinsic Value of the Shares

Dividing the PV of the FCFF and Terminal Value (the Value of the entire firm) by the number of outstanding shares we get the per share intrinsic value. We can compare this price with the current market price of the stock to get the Discount or Premium to its intrinsic price.

Persistent Systems Valuation	Units
PV in INR Million	97579
No of Shares Outstanding (In Million)	80
Intrinsic Value	1219.73

BILLION DOLLAR VALUATION

Current Market Price of Share	1468
Current Discount/Premium	20%

Persistent Systems Valuation and Intrinsic Share Price = INR 1219.73

DCF Valuation

MAHINDRA CIE VALUATION

Mahindra CIE is a multi-technology automotive components supplier and a subsidiary of the CIE Automotive group of Spain. They are an industrial group specialised in supplying components and subassemblies for the automotive market, which has presence across the globe and is listed on the stock exchanges in Madrid and Bilbao. The company in India manufactures shafts, couplings, gears, thermosets, composites etc and is India's Leading Producer of Magnets for Automotive Applications. From here, we go ahead with Mahindra CIE Valuation and Intrinsic Value of its shares.

Read more here: **Mahindra CIE Shares Fundamental Analysis**
Methodology Used:
Discounted cash flow (DCF) is a valuation method used to estimate the value of an investment based on its expected future cash flows. DCF analysis attempts to figure out the value of an investment today, based on projections of how much money it will generate in the future. The following step by step procedure is followed.

1. Determining the Revenue Growth Rates
2. Forecasting the Financial Statements
3. Deriving the FCFF and FCFE
4. Calculating the Terminal Value
5. Calculating the Discount Rate

6. Discounting the Cashflows
7. Arriving at the Intrinsic Value of the Shares

Step 1: Determining the Revenue Growth Rates

We arrive at the below table by using the past and expected future performance of both the company and the economy. This along with adjustments to changes in the management expectations, extraordinary events and other macro factors give the revenue growth rates for Mahindra CIE Valuation.

Financial Year	Revenue Growth Rate
Year 1	-2%
Year 2	-23%
Year 3	22%
Year 4	19%
Year 5	15%

Step 2: Forecasting the Financial Statements

The financial statements are forecasted for a period of 5 years using the annual report data of the company. The assumptions used for forecasting are tabulated below. The Excel model is completely editable and can be adjusted for specific changes which may happen over a period of time.

Assumptions Control Sheet	
Income Statement	
Average COGS as Percentage of Revenue	43.76%
Research and Development as Percentage of Revenue	0.00%
Sales, General and administrative as Percentage of Revenue	0.85%
Other operating expenses as Percentage of Revenue	45.00%
Other income (expense) as Percentage of Revenue	-0.57%
Balance Sheet	
Short Term Debt as Percentage of Total Assets	5.37%
Long Term Debt as Percentage of Total Assets	15.97%
Cash and Cash Equivalents as Percentage of Revenue	1.52%
Short Term Equivalents as Percentage of Revenue	3.16%
Accounts Receivables as Percentage of Revenue	8.64%
Inventory as Percentage of Revenue	14.71%
Prepaid Expenses as Percentage of Revenue	1.06%
Other Current Assets as Percentage of Revenue	2.77%
Gross property, plant and equipment as Percentage of Revenue	45.89%
Intangible assets as Percentage of Revenue	0.19%
Other long-term assets as Percentage of Revenue	4.73%
Accounts payable as Percentage of Revenue	21.85%
Corporate Tax Rate	22.00%
Other current liabilities as Percentage of Revenue	3.26%
Retained Earnings as as Percentage of Net Income	99.54%
Accumulated other comprehensive income as Percentage of Revenue	23.05%
Cashflow Statement	
Other Working Capital as Percentage of Revenue	0.52%

Step 3: Deriving the FCFF and FCFE

Free cash flow to the firm (FCFF) represents the amount of cash flow from operations available for distribution after accounting for depreciation expenses, taxes, working capital, and investments. FCFF is a measurement of a company's profitability after all expenses and reinvestments. It is given as follows.

Free cash flow to equity (FCFE) is a measure of how much cash is available to the equity shareholders of a company after all expenses, reinvestment, and debt are paid. FCFE is a measure of equity capital usage.

F/S Items (INR Millions)	Mar-20	Mar-21	Mar-22	Mar-23	Mar-24
Free Cash Flow to Firm	9204	10170	1680	2743	4297

| Free Cash Flow to Equity | 9841 | 6736 | 2551 | 3599 | 4925 |

Step 4: Calculating the Terminal Value

Terminal value (TV) is the value of a business or project beyond the forecast period when future cash flows can be estimated. It assumes that a business will grow at a set growth rate forever after the forecast period. Terminal value often comprises a large percentage of the total assessed value.

Terminal Value Calculation	Units INR Millions
Free Cash Flow to Firm	4296.60
Growth Rate	5.00%
Cost of Capital	13.24%
Terminal Value	54783.16

Step 5: Calculating the Discount Rate

DCF analysis helps assess the viability of a project or investment by calculating the present value of expected future cash flows using a discount rate. Here we use the Weighted average cost of capital (WACC) to discount the cash flow. The below table from the excel model shows the calculation of WACC for Mahindra CIE Valuation.

Cost of Equity Calcuation using CAPM	
Risk Free Rate (5 year G-Sec)	5.18%
Stock Beta (Ref: Reuters)	1.13
Beta Unlevered B/(1+ D(1-t)/E)	0.87
Beta Relevered B*(1+ D(1-t)/E)	1.08
Market Return Rm (Nifty 50 10 Year CAGR)	14.25%
Cost of Equity	**14.96%**

Cost of Debt	
Cost of Debt (Interest Expense/Total Debt)	**7.49%**

Cost of Capital	
Cost of Equity	14.96%
Weight of Equity in Target Capital Structure	76.89%
Cost of Debt	7.49%
Weight of Debt in Capital Structure	23.11%
WACC	**13.24%**

Step 6: Discounting the Cashflows

The WACC and the Cost of Equity for the company calculated in the above step are then used to discount the FCFF, FCFE and Terminal Value calculated in Step 3 and 4. In our case, we'll only consider the FCFF based Intrinsic price of the shares as it represents the cash flow to all the suppliers of capital and not only to the equity shareholders. Thus we arrive at Present value of future FCFF for Mahindra CIE Valuation. (Units are INR Millions)

FCFF Calculation	FV	Discounted
Mar-20	9204.49	8128.66
Mar-21	10170.05	7931.61
Mar-22	1679.63	1156.83
Mar-23	2742.98	1668.40
Mar-24	4296.60	2307.92
Terminal Value	54783.16	29426.75
Present Value (PV)		50620.16

FCFE Calculation	FV	Discounted
Mar-20	9841.02	8560.26
Mar-21	6735.89	5096.69
Mar-22	2550.52	1678.68
Mar-23	3599.05	2060.50
Mar-24	4924.99	2452.66
Terminal Value	54783.16	27282.24
Present Value (PV)		47131.04

Step 7: Arriving at the Intrinsic Value of the Shares

Dividing the PV of the FCFF and Terminal Value (the Value of the entire firm) by the number of outstanding shares we get the per share intrinsic value. We can compare this price with the current market price of the stock to get the Discount or Premium to its intrinsic price.

Mahindra CIE Valuation	Units
PV in INR Million	50620
No of Shares Outstanding (In Million)	379
Intrinsic Value	133.56

Current Market Price of Share	163
Current Discount/Premium	22%

Mahindra CIE Valuation and Intrinsic Share Price = INR 133.56

DCF Valuation

VODAFONE IDEA VALUATION

Vodafone Idea is an Indian telecom operator with its headquarters in Mumbai and Gandhinagar. The company is a pan-India integrated GSM operator offering 2G, 3G and 4G, 4G+ and VoLTE. Vodafone Idea various service brands are "Vodafone" – a postpaid & Prepaid GSM service and "Idea", which is a prepaid GSM service, similar to Vodafone Prepaid. From here, we go ahead with Vodafone Idea Valuation and Intrinsic Value of its shares.

Read more here: Vodafone Idea Shares Fundamental Analysis
Methodology Used:
Discounted cash flow (DCF) is a valuation method used to estimate the value of an investment based on its expected future cash flows. DCF analysis attempts to figure out the value of an investment today, based on projections of how much money it will generate in the future. The following step by step procedure is followed.

1. Determining the Revenue Growth Rates
2. Forecasting the Financial Statements
3. Deriving the FCFF and FCFE
4. Calculating the Terminal Value
5. Calculating the Discount Rate
6. Discounting the Cashflows
7. Arriving at the Intrinsic Value of the Shares

Step 1: Determining the Revenue Growth Rates
We arrive at the below table by using the past and expected fu-

ture performance of both the company and the economy. This along with adjustments to changes in the management expectations, extraordinary events and other macro factors give the revenue growth rates for Vodafone Idea Valuation.

Financial Year	Revenue Growth Rate
Year 1	21%
Year 2	-14%
Year 3	16%
Year 4	15%
Year 5	18%

Step 2: Forecasting the Financial Statements

The financial statements are forecasted for a period of 5 years using the annual report data of the company. The assumptions used for forecasting are tabulated below. The Excel model is completely editable and can be adjusted for specific changes which may happen over a period of time.

Assumptions Control Sheet

Income Statement	
Average COGS as Percentage of Revenue	55.60%
Research and Development as Percentage of Revenue	0.00%
Sales, General and administrative as Percentage of Revenue	11.26%
Other operating expenses as Percentage of Revenue	31.26%
Other income (expense) as Percentage of Revenue	2.15%
Balance Sheet	
Short Term Debt as Percentage of Total Assets	7.19%
Long Term Debt as Percentage of Total Assets	46.98%
Cash and Cash Equivalents as Percentage of Revenue	1.93%
Short Term Equivalents as Percentage of Revenue	17.89%
Accounts Receivables as Percentage of Revenue	3.01%
Inventory as Percentage of Revenue	0.16%
Prepaid Expenses as Percentage of Revenue	1.66%
Other Current Assets as Percentage of Revenue	8.84%
Gross property, plant and equipment as Percentage of Revenue	125.71%
Intangible assets as Percentage of Revenue	188.02%
Other long-term assets as Percentage of Revenue	21.69%
Accounts payable as Percentage of Revenue	15.74%
Corporate Tax Rate	22.00%
Other current liabilities as Percentage of Revenue	25.01%
Retained Earnings as as Percentage of Net Income	181.14%
Accumulated other comprehensive Income as Percentage of Revenue	-22.89%
Cashflow Statement	
Other Working Capital as Percentage of Revenue	-1.89%

Step 3: Deriving the FCFF and FCFE

Free cash flow to the firm (FCFF) represents the amount of cash flow from operations available for distribution after accounting for depreciation expenses, taxes, working capital, and investments. FCFF is a measurement of a company's profitability after all expenses and reinvestments. It is given as follows.

Free cash flow to equity (FCFE) is a measure of how much cash is available to the equity shareholders of a company after all expenses, reinvestment, and debt are paid. FCFE is a measure of equity capital usage.

F/S Items (INR Millions)	Mar-20	Mar-21	Mar-22	Mar-23	Mar-24
Free Cash Flow to Firm	3940	21838	30695	27028	30347

| Free Cash Flow to Equity | -477369 | -94497 | 253050 | 263176 | 341501 |

Step 4: Calculating the Terminal Value

Terminal value (TV) is the value of a business or project beyond the forecast period when future cash flows can be estimated. It assumes that a business will grow at a set growth rate forever after the forecast period. Terminal value often comprises a large percentage of the total assessed value.

Terminal Value Calculation	Units INR Millions
Free Cash Flow to Firm	30346.79
Growth Rate	4.00%
Cost of Capital	24.36%
Terminal Value	155001.62

Step 5: Calculating the Discount Rate

DCF analysis helps assess the viability of a project or investment by calculating the present value of expected future cash flows using a discount rate. Here we use the Weighted average cost of capital (WACC) to discount the cash flow. The below table from the excel model shows the calculation of WACC for Vodafone Idea Valuation.

Cost of Equity Calcuation using CAPM	
Risk Free Rate (5 year G-Sec)	5.18%
Stock Beta (Ref: Reuters)	1.12
Beta Unlevered B/(1+ D(1-t)/E)	0.42
Beta Relevered B*(1+ D(1-t)/E)	70.35
Market Return Rm (Nifty 50 10 Year CAGR)	14.25%
Cost of Equity	**643.24%**

Cost of Debt	
Cost of Debt (Interest Expense/Total Debt)	5.22%

Cost of Capital	
Cost of Equity	643.24%
Weight of Equity in Target Capital Structure	3.00%
Cost of Debt	5.22%
Weight of Debt in Capital Structure	97.00%
WACC	**24.36%**

Step 6: Discounting the Cashflows

The WACC and the Cost of Equity for the company calculated in the above step are then used to discount the FCFF, FCFE and Terminal Value calculated in Step 3 and 4. In our case, we'll only consider the FCFF based Intrinsic price of the shares as it represents the cash flow to all the suppliers of capital and not only to the equity shareholders. Thus we arrive at Present value of future FCFF for Vodafone Idea Valuation. (Units are INR Millions)

FCFF Calculation	FV	Discounted
Mar-20	3939.93	3168.13
Mar-21	21837.71	14120.02
Mar-22	30695.22	15959.26
Mar-23	27027.62	11299.62
Mar-24	30346.79	10201.94
Terminal Value	155001.62	52108.24
Present Value (PV)		106857.22

FCFE Calculation	FV	Discounted
Mar-20	-477368.78	-64227.74
Mar-21	-94496.99	-1710.63
Mar-22	253050.39	616.33
Mar-23	263176.33	86.24
Mar-24	341500.80	15.06
Terminal Value	155001.62	6.83
Present Value (PV)		-65213.90

Step 7: Arriving at the Intrinsic Value of the Shares

Dividing the PV of the FCFF and Terminal Value (the Value of the entire firm) by the number of outstanding shares we get the per share intrinsic value. We can compare this price with the current market price of the stock to get the Discount or Premium to its intrinsic price.

Vodafone Idea Valuation	Units
PV in INR Million	106857
No of Shares Outstanding (In Million)	6913
Intrinsic Value	15.46

BILLION DOLLAR VALUATION

| Current Market Price of Share | 10.10 |
| Current Discount/Premium | -35% |

Vodafone Idea Valuation and Intrinsic Share Price = INR 15.46

ONGC VALUATION

ONGC is the largest crude oil and natural gas company in India. The company contributes around 75% of the total domestic production and has Maharatna status bestowed by the Indian Government. This extracted crude oil is then used as a raw material by downstream companies like IOC, BPCL, and HPCL (a subsidiary of ONGC) to produce petroleum products like Petrol, Diesel, Kerosene, Naphtha, and Cooking Gas-LPG. From here, we go ahead with ONGC Valuation and Intrinsic Value of its shares.

Read more here: ONGC Shares Fundamental Analysis

Methodology Used:

Discounted cash flow (DCF) is a valuation method used to estimate the value of an investment based on its expected future cash flows. DCF analysis attempts to figure out the value of an investment today, based on projections of how much money it will generate in the future. The following step by step procedure is followed.

1. Determining the Revenue Growth Rates
2. Forecasting the Financial Statements
3. Deriving the FCFF and FCFE
4. Calculating the Terminal Value
5. Calculating the Discount Rate
6. Discounting the Cashflows
7. Arriving at the Intrinsic Value of the Shares

Step 1: Determining the Revenue Growth Rates

We arrive at the below table by using the past and expected future performance of both the company and the economy. This along with adjustments to changes in the management expectations, extraordinary events and other macro factors give the revenue growth rates for ONGC Valuation.

Financial Year	Revenue Growth Rate
Year 1	-6%
Year 2	-26%
Year 3	19%
Year 4	17%
Year 5	15%

Step 2: Forecasting the Financial Statements

The financial statements are forecasted for a period of 5 years using the annual report data of the company. The assumptions used for forecasting are tabulated below. The Excel model is completely editable and can be adjusted for specific changes which may happen over a period of time.

Assumptions Control Sheet	
Income Statement	
Average COGS as Percentage of Revenue	72.28%
Research and Development as Percentage of Revenue	0.22%
Sales, General and administrative as Percentage of Revenue	3.08%
Other operating expenses as Percentage of Revenue	10.88%
Other income (expense) as Percentage of Revenue	1.44%
Balance Sheet	
Short Term Debt as Percentage of Total Assets	6.87%
Long Term Debt as Percentage of Total Assets	11.15%
Cash and Cash Equivalents as Percentage of Revenue	0.99%
Short Term Equivalents as Percentage of Revenue	3.26%
Accounts Receivables as Percentage of Revenue	5.14%
Inventory as Percentage of Revenue	8.85%
Prepaid Expenses as Percentage of Revenue	1.60%
Other Current Assets as Percentage of Revenue	7.33%
Gross property, plant and equipment as Percentage of Revenue	95.96%
Intangible assets as Percentage of Revenue	14.15%
Other long-term assets as Percentage of Revenue	31.05%
Accounts payable as Percentage of Revenue	10.68%
Corporate Tax Rate	22.00%
Other current liabilities as Percentage of Revenue	13.80%
Retained Earnings as as Percentage of Net Income	8.50%
Accumulated other comprehensive income as Percentage of Revenue	66.90%
Cashflow Statement	
Other Working Capital as Percentage of Revenue	0.88%

Step 3: Deriving the FCFF and FCFE

Free cash flow to the firm (FCFF) represents the amount of cash flow from operations available for distribution after accounting for depreciation expenses, taxes, working capital, and investments. FCFF is a measurement of a company's profitability after all expenses and reinvestments. It is given as follows.

Free cash flow to equity (FCFE) is a measure of how much cash is available to the equity shareholders of a company after all expenses, reinvestment, and debt are paid. FCFE is a measure of equity capital usage.

F/S Items (INR Millions)	Mar-20	Mar-21	Mar-22	Mar-23	Mar-24
Free Cash Flow to Firm	175735	34519	102514	181406	254470

| Free Cash Flow to Equity | 562927 | -1183294 | 617011 | 737303 | 829843 |

Step 4: Calculating the Terminal Value

Terminal value (TV) is the value of a business or project beyond the forecast period when future cash flows can be estimated. It assumes that a business will grow at a set growth rate forever after the forecast period. Terminal value often comprises a large percentage of the total assessed value.

Terminal Value Calculation	Units INR Millions
Free Cash Flow to Firm	254469.62
Growth Rate	5.00%
Cost of Capital	11.76%
Terminal Value	3951017.93

Step 5: Calculating the Discount Rate

DCF analysis helps assess the viability of a project or investment by calculating the present value of expected future cash flows using a discount rate. Here we use the Weighted average cost of capital (WACC) to discount the cash flow. The below table from the excel model shows the calculation of WACC for ONGC Valuation.

Cost of Equity Calcuation using CAPM	
Risk Free Rate (5 year G-Sec)	5.18%
Stock Beta (Ref: Reuters)	1.24
Beta Unlevered B/(1+ D(1-t)/E)	0.90
Beta Relevered B*(1+ D(1-t)/E)	1.54
Market Return Rm (Nifty 50 10 Year CAGR)	14.25%
Cost of Equity	**19.15%**

Cost of Debt	
Cost of Debt (Interest Expense/Total Debt)	**3.73%**

Cost of Capital	
Cost of Equity	19.15%
Weight of Equity in Target Capital Structure	52.08%
Cost of Debt	3.73%
Weight of Debt in Capital Structure	47.92%
WACC	**11.76%**

Step 6: Discounting the Cashflows

The WACC and the Cost of Equity for the company calculated in the above step are then used to discount the FCFF, FCFE and Terminal Value calculated in Step 3 and 4. In our case, we'll only consider the FCFF based Intrinsic price of the shares as it represents the cash flow to all the suppliers of capital and not only to the equity shareholders. Thus we arrive at Present value of future FCFF for ONGC Valuation. (Units are INR Millions)

FCFF Calculation	FV	Discounted
Mar-20	175735.40	157239.84
Mar-21	34519.23	27635.53
Mar-22	102514.42	73433.63
Mar-23	181406.10	116269.36
Mar-24	254469.62	145932.72
Terminal Value	3951017.93	2265821.80
Present Value (PV)		2786332.89

FCFE Calculation	FV	Discounted
Mar-20	562927.37	472450.69
Mar-21	-1183294.32	-833491.22
Mar-22	617011.14	364758.46
Mar-23	737303.05	365815.85
Mar-24	829843.29	345554.62
Terminal Value	3951017.93	1645241.34
Present Value (PV)		2360329.74

Step 7: Arriving at the Intrinsic Value of the Shares

Dividing the PV of the FCFF and Terminal Value (the value of the entire firm) by the number of outstanding shares we get the per-share intrinsic value. We can compare this price with the current market price of the stock to get the Discount or Premium to its intrinsic price.

ONGC Valuation	Units
PV in INR Million	2786333
No of Shares Outstanding (In Million)	12807
Intrinsic Value	217.56

Current Market Price of Share	94.00
Current Discount/Premium	-57%

ONGC Valuation and Intrinsic Share Price = INR 217.56

DCF Valuation

TRIDENT VALUATION

Trident Ltd is the largest manufacturer of terry towels in the world. It is a flagship company of the US $ 1 billion Indian business conglomerate and global player, Trident Group which is headquartered in Ludhiana, Punjab. Over the years Trident has evolved into one of the world's largest integrated home textile manufacturer. The Company is engaged in the business of manufacturing a wide variety of yarn, bed, bath linen, paper and chemicals. From here, we go ahead with Trident Valuation and Intrinsic Value of its shares.

Read more here: Trident Shares Fundamental Analysis

Methodology Used:

Discounted cash flow (DCF) is a valuation method used to estimate the value of an investment based on its expected future cash flows. DCF analysis attempts to figure out the value of an investment today, based on projections of how much money it will generate in the future. The following step by step procedure is followed.

1. Determining the Revenue Growth Rates
2. Forecasting the Financial Statements
3. Deriving the FCFF and FCFE
4. Calculating the Terminal Value
5. Calculating the Discount Rate
6. Discounting the Cashflows
7. Arriving at the Intrinsic Value of the Shares

Step 1: Determining the Revenue Growth Rates

We arrive at the below table by using the past and expected future performance of both the company and the economy. This along with adjustments to changes in the management expectations, extraordinary events and other macro factors give the revenue growth rates for Trident Valuation.

Financial Year	Revenue Growth Rate
Year 1	-12%
Year 2	6%
Year 3	18%
Year 4	17%
Year 5	15%

Step 2: Forecasting the Financial Statements

The financial statements are forecasted for a period of 5 years using the annual report data of the company. The assumptions used for forecasting are tabulated below. The Excel model is completely editable and can be adjusted for specific changes which may happen over a period of time.

Assumptions Control Sheet

Income Statement	
Average COGS as Percentage of Revenue	50.51%
Research and Development as Percentage of Revenue	0.00%
Sales, General and administrative as Percentage of Revenue	1.73%
Other operating expenses as Percentage of Revenue	36.71%
Other income (expense) as Percentage of Revenue	0.70%
Balance Sheet	
Short Term Debt as Percentage of Total Assets	20.61%
Long Term Debt as Percentage of Total Assets	25.27%
Cash and Cash Equivalents as Percentage of Revenue	1.33%
Short Term Equivalents as Percentage of Revenue	1.40%
Accounts Receivables as Percentage of Revenue	9.35%
Inventory as Percentage of Revenue	20.22%
Prepaid Expenses as Percentage of Revenue	0.75%
Other Current Assets as Percentage of Revenue	5.59%
Gross property, plant and equipment as Percentage of Revenue	112.93%
Intangible assets as Percentage of Revenue	0.00%
Other long-term assets as Percentage of Revenue	5.21%
Accounts payable as Percentage of Revenue	4.50%
Corporate Tax Rate	22.00%
Other current liabilities as Percentage of Revenue	4.26%
Retained Earnings as as Percentage of Net Income	57.58%
Accumulated other comprehensive income as Percentage of Revenue	25.81%
Cashflow Statement	
Other Working Capital as Percentage of Revenue	1.26%

Step 3: Deriving the FCFF and FCFE

Free cash flow to the firm (FCFF) represents the amount of cash flow from operations available for distribution after accounting for depreciation expenses, taxes, working capital, and investments. FCFF is a measurement of a company's profitability after all expenses and reinvestments. It is given as follows.

Free cash flow to equity (FCFE) is a measure of how much cash is available to the equity shareholders of a company after all expenses, reinvestment, and debt are paid. FCFE is a measure of equity capital usage.

F/S Items (INR Millions)	Mar-20	Mar-21	Mar-22	Mar-23	Mar-24
Free Cash Flow to Firm	-1677	-314	3231	4702	5898

| Free Cash Flow to Equity | 5758 | -281 | 3766 | 5560 | 7018 |

Step 4: Calculating the Terminal Value

Terminal value (TV) is the value of a business or project beyond the forecast period when future cash flows can be estimated. It assumes that a business will grow at a set growth rate forever after the forecast period. Terminal value often comprises a large percentage of the total assessed value.

Terminal Value Calculation	Units INR Millions
Free Cash Flow to Firm	5897.55
Growth Rate	4.00%
Cost of Capital	9.98%
Terminal Value	102568.41

Step 5: Calculating the Discount Rate

DCF analysis helps assess the viability of a project or investment by calculating the present value of expected future cash flows using a discount rate. Here we use the Weighted average cost of capital (WACC) to discount the cash flow. The below table from the excel model shows the calculation of WACC for Trident Valuation.

Cost of Equity Calcuation using CAPM	
Risk Free Rate (5 year G-Sec)	5.18%
Stock Beta (Ref: Reuters)	0.86
Beta Unlevered B/(1+ D(1-t)/E)	0.52
Beta Relevered B*(1+ D(1-t)/E)	0.98
Market Return Rm (Nifty 50 10 Year CAGR)	14.25%
Cost of Equity	**14.09%**

Cost of Debt	
Cost of Debt (Interest Expense/Total Debt)	6.30%

Cost of Capital	
Cost of Equity	14.09%
Weight of Equity in Target Capital Structure	47.23%
Cost of Debt	6.30%
Weight of Debt in Capital Structure	52.77%
WACC	**9.98%**

Step 6: Discounting the Cashflows

The WACC and the Cost of Equity for the company calculated in the above step are then used to discount the FCFF, FCFE and Terminal Value calculated in Step 3 and 4. In our case, we'll only consider the FCFF based Intrinsic price of the shares as it represents the cash flow to all the suppliers of capital and not only to the equity shareholders. Thus we arrive at Present value of future FCFF for Trident Valuation. (Units are INR Millions)

STOCK VALUATION HANDBOOK PART 2

FCFF Calculation	FV	Discounted
Mar-20	-1677.15	-1524.96
Mar-21	-313.70	-259.35
Mar-22	3231.00	2428.83
Mar-23	4701.78	3213.73
Mar-24	5897.55	3665.27
Terminal Value	102568.41	63745.23
Present Value (PV)		71268.75

FCFE Calculation	FV	Discounted
Mar-20	5757.91	5046.96
Mar-21	-280.77	-215.71
Mar-22	3765.58	2535.86
Mar-23	5560.31	3282.14
Mar-24	7018.00	3631.09
Terminal Value	102568.41	53068.51
Present Value (PV)		67348.84

Step 7: Arriving at the Intrinsic Value of the Shares

Dividing the PV of the FCFF and Terminal Value (the Value of the entire firm) by the number of outstanding shares we get the per share intrinsic value. We can compare this price with the current market price of the stock to get the Discount or Premium to its intrinsic price.

Trident Valuation	Units
PV in INR Million	71269
No of Shares Outstanding (In Million)	4981
Intrinsic Value	14.31

Current Market Price of Share	9.37
Current Discount/Premium	-35%

Trident Valuation and Intrinsic Share Price = INR 14.31

DCF Valuation

ESSEL PROPACK VALUATION

Essel Propack is the part of the Indian business conglomerate Essel Group, with headquarters in Mumbai. The company is the largest global speciality packaging company in the world. It operates in five major packaging segments namely Beauty and Cosmetics, Pharma and Health, Food, Home and Oral care. The company is focused on developing innovative packaging solution for more than 400+ companies across the world. From here, we go ahead with Essel Propack Valuation and Intrinsic Value of its shares.

Read more here: Essel Propack Shares Fundamental Analysis
Methodology Used:
Discounted cash flow (DCF) is a valuation method used to estimate the value of an investment based on its expected future cash flows. DCF analysis attempts to figure out the value of an investment today, based on projections of how much money it will generate in the future. The following step by step procedure is followed.

1. Determining the Revenue Growth Rates
2. Forecasting the Financial Statements
3. Deriving the FCFF and FCFE
4. Calculating the Terminal Value
5. Calculating the Discount Rate
6. Discounting the Cashflows

7. Arriving at the Intrinsic Value of the Shares

Step 1: Determining the Revenue Growth Rates

We arrive at the below table by using the past and expected future performance of both the company and the economy. This along with adjustments to changes in the management expectations, extraordinary events and other macro factors give the revenue growth rates for Essel Propack Valuation.

Financial Year	Revenue Growth Rate
Year 1	-40%
Year 2	15%
Year 3	16%
Year 4	13%
Year 5	13%

Step 2: Forecasting the Financial Statements

The financial statements are forecasted for a period of 5 years using the annual report data of the company. The assumptions used for forecasting are tabulated below. The Excel model is completely editable and can be adjusted for specific changes which may happen over a period of time.

Assumptions Control Sheet	
Income Statement	
Average COGS as Percentage of Revenue	45.51%
Research and Development as Percentage of Revenue	0.00%
Sales, General and administrative as Percentage of Revenue	4.05%
Other operating expenses as Percentage of Revenue	37.90%
Other income (expense) as Percentage of Revenue	0.35%
Balance Sheet	
Short Term Debt as Percentage of Total Assets	7.39%
Long Term Debt as Percentage of Total Assets	23.47%
Cash and Cash Equivalents as Percentage of Revenue	4.11%
Short Term Equivalents as Percentage of Revenue	1.69%
Accounts Receivables as Percentage of Revenue	17.14%
Inventory as Percentage of Revenue	10.80%
Prepaid Expenses as Percentage of Revenue	4.02%
Other Current Assets as Percentage of Revenue	6.09%
Gross property, plant and equipment as Percentage of Revenue	61.32%
Intangible assets as Percentage of Revenue	1.70%
Other long-term assets as Percentage of Revenue	3.67%
Accounts payable as Percentage of Revenue	6.98%
Corporate Tax Rate	22.00%
Other current liabilities as Percentage of Revenue	8.98%
Retained Earnings as as Percentage of Net Income	77.66%
Accumulated other comprehensive income as Percentage of Revenue	31.17%
Cashflow Statement	
Other Working Capital as Percentage of Revenue	-0.36%

Step 3: Deriving the FCFF and FCFE

Free cash flow to the firm (FCFF) represents the amount of cash flow from operations available for distribution after accounting for depreciation expenses, taxes, working capital, and investments. FCFF is a measurement of a company's profitability after all expenses and reinvestments. It is given as follows.

Free cash flow to equity (FCFE) is a measure of how much cash is available to the equity shareholders of a company after all expenses, reinvestment, and debt are paid. FCFE is a measure of equity capital usage.

F/S Items (INR Millions)	Mar-20	Mar-21	Mar-22	Mar-23	Mar-24
Free Cash Flow	602	784	1034	1191	1821

to Firm					
Free Cash Flow to Equity	1830	808	1166	1355	2076

Step 4: Calculating the Terminal Value

Terminal value (TV) is the value of a business or project beyond the forecast period when future cash flows can be estimated. It assumes that a business will grow at a set growth rate forever after the forecast period. Terminal value often comprises a large percentage of the total assessed value.

Terminal Value Calculation	Units INR Millions
Free Cash Flow to Firm	1821.19
Growth Rate	5.00%
Cost of Capital	11.6%
Terminal Value	28993.97

Step 5: Calculating the Discount Rate

DCF analysis helps assess the viability of a project or investment by calculating the present value of expected future cash flows using a discount rate. Here we use the Weighted average cost of capital (WACC) to discount the cash flow. The below table from the excel model shows the calculation of WACC for Essel Propack Valuation.

Cost of Equity Calcuation using CAPM	
Risk Free Rate (5 year G-Sec)	5.18%
Stock Beta (Ref: Reuters)	0.90
Beta Unlevered B/(1+ D(1-t)/E)	0.66
Beta Relevered B*(1+ D(1-t)/E)	0.97
Market Return Rm (Nifty 50 10 Year CAGR)	14.25%
Cost of Equity	**13.95%**

Cost of Debt	
Cost of Debt (Interest Expense/Total Debt)	7.56%

Cost of Capital	
Cost of Equity	13.95%
Weight of Equity in Target Capital Structure	63.11%
Cost of Debt	7.56%
Weight of Debt in Capital Structure	36.89%
WACC	**11.60%**

Step 6: Discounting the Cashflows

The WACC and the Cost of Equity for the company calculated in the above step are then used to discount the FCFF, FCFE and Terminal Value calculated in Step 3 and 4. In our case, we'll only consider the FCFF based Intrinsic price of the shares as it represents the cash flow to all the suppliers of capital and not only to the equity shareholders. Thus we arrive at Present value of future FCFF for Essel Propack Valuation. (Units are INR Millions)

FCFF Calculation	FV	Discounted
Mar-20	602.30	539.72
Mar-21	783.63	629.25
Mar-22	1033.53	743.68
Mar-23	1190.91	767.88
Mar-24	1821.19	1052.26
Terminal Value	28993.97	16752.43
Present Value (PV)		20485.21

FCFE Calculation	FV	Discounted
Mar-20	1830.41	1606.29
Mar-21	807.69	622.01
Mar-22	1165.75	787.82
Mar-23	1355.45	803.86
Mar-24	2076.17	1080.53
Terminal Value	28993.97	15089.77
Present Value (PV)		19990.29

Step 7: Arriving at the Intrinsic Value of the Shares

Dividing the PV of the FCFF and Terminal Value (the Value of the entire firm) by the number of outstanding shares we get the per share intrinsic value. We can compare this price with the current market price of the stock to get the Discount or Premium to its intrinsic price.

Essel Propack Valuation	Units
PV in INR Million	20485
No of Shares Outstanding (In Million)	315
Intrinsic Value	188

Current Market Price of Share	264
Current Discount/Premium	29%

Essel Propack Valuation and Intrinsic Share Price = INR 188

L&T Shares DCF Valuation

L&T VALUATION

Larsen & Toubro, commonly known as L&T is India's largest engineering and construction company with interests in Projects, Infrastructure development, Manufacturing, IT and Financial services. It is one of Asia's largest vertically integrated Engineering Procurement and Construction (EPC) company and also a market leader in turnkey projects. Some of their well-known projects include the Statue of Unity in Gujrat, Mumbai International Airport, Petronas Refinery in Malaysia, Twin Towers in Dubai and Stadium at Barbados. From here, we go ahead with L&T Valuation and Intrinsic Value of its shares.

Read more here: L&T Shares Fundamental Analysis
Methodology Used:
Discounted cash flow (DCF) is a valuation method used to estimate the value of an investment based on its expected future cash flows. DCF analysis attempts to figure out the value of an investment today, based on projections of how much money it will generate in the future. The following step by step procedure is followed.

1. Determining the Revenue Growth Rates
2. Forecasting the Financial Statements
3. Deriving the FCFF and FCFE
4. Calculating the Terminal Value
5. Calculating the Discount Rate
6. Discounting the Cashflows
7. Arriving at the Intrinsic Value of the Shares

Step 1: Determining the Revenue Growth Rates

We arrive at the below table by using the past and expected future performance of both the company and the economy. This along with adjustments to changes in the management expectations, extraordinary events and other macro factors give the revenue growth rates for L&T Valuation.

Financial Year	Revenue Growth Rate
Year 1	5%
Year 2	-4%
Year 3	18%
Year 4	11%
Year 5	14%

Step 2: Forecasting the Financial Statements

The financial statements are forecasted for a period of 5 years using the annual report data of the company. The assumptions used for forecasting are tabulated below. The Excel model is completely editable and can be adjusted for specific changes which may happen over a period of time.

Assumptions Control Sheet	
Income Statement	
Average COGS as Percentage of Revenue	63.04%
Research and Development as Percentage of Revenue	0.00%
Sales, General and administrative as Percentage of Revenue	2.82%
Other operating expenses as Percentage of Revenue	24.60%
Other income (expense) as Percentage of Revenue	1.11%
Balance Sheet	
Short Term Debt as Percentage of Total Assets	14.87%
Long Term Debt as Percentage of Total Assets	29.85%
Cash and Cash Equivalents as Percentage of Revenue	4.85%
Short Term Equivalents as Percentage of Revenue	10.70%
Accounts Receivables as Percentage of Revenue	45.96%
Inventory as Percentage of Revenue	4.73%
Prepaid Expenses as Percentage of Revenue	0.35%
Other Current Assets as Percentage of Revenue	46.98%
Gross property, plant and equipment as Percentage of Revenue	14.51%
Intangible assets as Percentage of Revenue	10.38%
Other long-term assets as Percentage of Revenue	58.77%
Accounts payable as Percentage of Revenue	28.88%
Corporate Tax Rate	22.00%
Other current liabilities as Percentage of Revenue	29.19%
Retained Earnings as as Percentage of Net Income	79.99%
Accumulated other comprehensive income as Percentage of Revenue	12.03%
Cashflow Statement	
Other Working Capital as Percentage of Revenue	10.29%

Step 3: Deriving the FCFF and FCFE

Free cash flow to the firm (FCFF) represents the amount of cash flow from operations available for distribution after accounting for depreciation expenses, taxes, working capital, and investments. FCFF is a measurement of a company's profitability after all expenses and reinvestments. It is given as follows.

Free cash flow to equity (FCFE) is a measure of how much cash is available to the equity shareholders of a company after all expenses, reinvestment, and debt are paid. FCFE is a measure of equity capital usage.

F/S Items (INR Millions)	Mar-20	Mar-21	Mar-22	Mar-23	Mar-24
Free Cash Flow	24479	65250	113107	117706	141181

to Firm					
Free Cash Flow to Equity	-29188	-95579	345179	245036	347799

Step 4: Calculating the Terminal Value

Terminal value (TV) is the value of a business or project beyond the forecast period when future cash flows can be estimated. It assumes that a business will grow at a set growth rate forever after the forecast period. Terminal value often comprises a large percentage of the total assessed value.

Terminal Value Calculation	Units INR Millions
Free Cash Flow to Firm	141181.20
Growth Rate	5.00%
Cost of Capital	11.20%
Terminal Value	2390146.72

Step 5: Calculating the Discount Rate

DCF analysis helps assess the viability of a project or investment by calculating the present value of expected future cash flows using a discount rate. Here we use the Weighted average cost of capital (WACC) to discount the cash flow. The below table from the excel model shows the calculation of WACC for L&T Valuation.

Cost of Equity Calcuation using CAPM	
Risk Free Rate (5 year G-Sec)	5.18%
Stock Beta (Ref: Reuters)	1.74
Beta Unlevered B/(1+ D(1-t)/E)	0.68
Beta Relevered B*(1+ D(1-t)/E)	2.09
Market Return Rm (Nifty 50 10 Year CAGR)	14.25%
Cost of Equity	**24.13%**

Cost of Debt	
Cost of Debt (Interest Expense/Total Debt)	**6.37%**

Cost of Capital	
Cost of Equity	24.13%
Weight of Equity in Target Capital Structure	27.21%
Cost of Debt	6.37%
Weight of Debt in Capital Structure	72.79%
WACC	**11.20%**

Step 6: Discounting the Cashflows

The WACC and the Cost of Equity for the company calculated in the above step are then used to discount the FCFF, FCFE and Terminal Value calculated in Step 3 and 4. In our case, we'll only consider the FCFF based Intrinsic price of the shares as it represents the cash flow to all the suppliers of capital and not only to the equity shareholders. Thus we arrive at Present value of future FCFF for L&T Valuation. (Units are INR Millions)

FCFF Calculation	FV	Discounted
Mar-20	24478.82	22012.91
Mar-21	65249.58	52765.67
Mar-22	113106.95	82252.64
Mar-23	117705.52	76974.04
Mar-24	141181.20	83025.43
Terminal Value	2390146.72	1405590.53
Present Value (PV)		1722621.21

FCFE Calculation	FV	Discounted
Mar-20	-29187.65	-23513.65
Mar-21	-95579.09	-62030.45
Mar-22	345178.77	180470.86
Mar-23	245036.28	103208.25
Mar-24	347799.41	118014.09
Terminal Value	2390146.72	811016.29
Present Value (PV)		1127165.39

Step 7: Arriving at the Intrinsic Value of the Shares

Dividing the PV of the FCFF and Terminal Value (the Value of the entire firm) by the number of outstanding shares we get the per share intrinsic value. We can compare this price with the current market price of the stock to get the Discount or Premium to its intrinsic price.

L&T Valuation	Units
PV in INR Million	1722621
No of Shares Outstanding (In Million)	1402
Intrinsic Value	1228.69

Current Market Price of Share	1288.00
Current Discount/Premium	5%

L&T Valuation and Intrinsic Share Price = INR 1228.69

Jindal Steel and Power Valuation

JINDAL STEEL AND POWER VALUATION

Jindal Steel and Power Limited is an Indian steel and energy company based in Hisar. The company is a leading player in steel, power, mining, oil, gas and infrastructure in India. It is a part of the $ 22 billion OP Jindal Group and is continuously scaling its capacity utilization and efficiencies to capture opportunities across global markets. The company operates in the metals, mining and utility industry where market dominance comes through scale, level of integration, capacity and cost structure. From here, we go ahead with Jindal Steel and Power Valuation and Intrinsic Value of its shares.

Read more here: Jindal Steel and Power Shares Fundamental Analysis

Methodology Used:

Discounted cash flow (DCF) is a valuation method used to estimate the value of an investment based on its expected future cash flows. DCF analysis attempts to figure out the value of an investment today, based on projections of how much money it will generate in the future. The following step by step procedure is followed.

1. Determining the Revenue Growth Rates
2. Forecasting the Financial Statements
3. Deriving the FCFF and FCFE
4. Calculating the Terminal Value
5. Calculating the Discount Rate
6. Discounting the Cashflows

7. Arriving at the Intrinsic Value of the Shares

Step 1: Determining the Revenue Growth Rates
We arrive at the below table by using the past and expected future performance of both the company and the economy. This along with adjustments to changes in the management expectations, extraordinary events and other macro factors give the revenue growth rates for Jindal Steel and Power Valuation.

Financial Year	Revenue Growth Rate
Year 1	-5%
Year 2	3%
Year 3	15%
Year 4	8%
Year 5	5%

Step 2: Forecasting the Financial Statements
The financial statements are forecasted for a period of 5 years using the annual report data of the company. The assumptions used for forecasting are tabulated below. The Excel model is completely editable and can be adjusted for specific changes which may happen over a period of time.

Assumptions Control Sheet	
Income Statement	
Average COGS as Percentage of Revenue	71.41%
Research and Development as Percentage of Revenue	0.01%
Sales, General and administrative as Percentage of Revenue	3.18%
Other operating expenses as Percentage of Revenue	19.58%
Other income (expense) as Percentage of Revenue	-2.56%
Balance Sheet	
Short Term Debt as Percentage of Total Assets	15.00%
Long Term Debt as Percentage of Total Assets	50.00%
Cash and Cash Equivalents as Percentage of Revenue	1.53%
Short Term Equivalents as Percentage of Revenue	1.43%
Accounts Receivables as Percentage of Revenue	6.41%
Inventory as Percentage of Revenue	15.33%
Prepaid Expenses as Percentage of Revenue	12.95%
Other Current Assets as Percentage of Revenue	8.94%
Gross property, plant and equipment as Percentage of Revenue	263.70%
Intangible assets as Percentage of Revenue	13.91%
Other long-term assets as Percentage of Revenue	#DIV/0!
Accounts payable as Percentage of Revenue	11.05%
Corporate Tax Rate	22.00%
Other current liabilities as Percentage of Revenue	15.75%
Retained Earnings as as Percentage of Net Income	121.15%
Accumulated other comprehensive income as Percentage of Revenue	16.87%
Cashflow Statement	
Other Working Capital as Percentage of Revenue	-2.66%

Step 3: Deriving the FCFF and FCFE

Free cash flow to the firm (FCFF) represents the amount of cash flow from operations available for distribution after accounting for depreciation expenses, taxes, working capital, and investments. FCFF is a measurement of a company's profitability after all expenses and reinvestments. It is given as follows.

Free cash flow to equity (FCFE) is a measure of how much cash is available to the equity shareholders of a company after all expenses, reinvestment, and debt are paid. FCFE is a measure of equity capital usage.

F/S Items (INR Millions)	Mar-20	Mar-21	Mar-22	Mar-23	Mar-24
Free Cash Flow	22430	33119	36746	39557	42884

to Firm					
Free Cash Flow to Equity	402096	-81430	-37697	-38041	-29751

Step 4: Calculating the Terminal Value

Terminal value (TV) is the value of a business or project beyond the forecast period when future cash flows can be estimated. It assumes that a business will grow at a set growth rate forever after the forecast period. Terminal value often comprises a large percentage of the total assessed value.

Terminal Value Calculation	Units INR Millions
Free Cash Flow to Firm	42884.13
Growth Rate	5.00%
Cost of Capital	14.23%
Terminal Value	488054.59

Step 5: Calculating the Discount Rate

DCF analysis helps assess the viability of a project or investment by calculating the present value of expected future cash flows using a discount rate. Here we use the Weighted average cost of capital (WACC) to discount the cash flow. The below table from the excel model shows the calculation of WACC for Jindal Steel and Power Valuation.

Cost of Equity Calcuation using CAPM	
Risk Free Rate (5 year G-Sec)	5.18%
Stock Beta (Ref: Reuters)	1.85
Beta Unlevered B/(1+ D(1-t)/E)	0.95
Beta Relevered B*(1+ D(1-t)/E)	4.41
Market Return Rm (Nifty 50 10 Year CAGR)	14.25%
Cost of Equity	**45.14%**

Cost of Debt	
Cost of Debt (Interest Expense/Total Debt)	7.62%

Cost of Capital	
Cost of Equity	45.14%
Weight of Equity in Target Capital Structure	17.62%
Cost of Debt	7.62%
Weight of Debt in Capital Structure	82.38%
WACC	**14.23%**

Step 6: Discounting the Cashflows

The WACC and the Cost of Equity for the company calculated in the above step are then used to discount the FCFF, FCFE and Terminal Value calculated in Step 3 and 4. In our case, we'll only consider the FCFF based Intrinsic price of the shares as it represents the cash flow to all the suppliers of capital and not only to the equity shareholders. Thus we arrive at Present value of future FCFF for Jindal Steel and Power Valuation. (Units are INR Millions)

FCFF Calculation	FV	Discounted
Mar-20	22429.99	19636.49
Mar-21	33118.56	25382.88
Mar-22	36745.60	24655.25
Mar-23	39557.06	23236.08
Mar-24	42884.13	22053.12
Terminal Value	488054.59	250981.63
Present Value (PV)		365945.44

FCFE Calculation	FV	Discounted
Mar-20	402096.50	277045.43
Mar-21	-81430.07	-38656.83
Mar-22	-37697.06	-12330.19
Mar-23	-38041.15	-8573.07
Mar-24	-29750.63	-4619.55
Terminal Value	488054.59	75783.03
Present Value (PV)		288648.82

Step 7: Arriving at the Intrinsic Value of the Shares

Dividing the PV of the FCFF and Terminal Value (the Value of the entire firm) by the number of outstanding shares we get the per share intrinsic value. We can compare this price with the current market price of the stock to get the Discount or Premium to its intrinsic price.

Jindal Steel and Power Valuation	Units
PV in INR Million	365945
No of Shares Outstanding (In Million)	968
Intrinsic Value	378.04

STOCK VALUATION HANDBOOK PART 2

Current Market Price of Share	233.00
Current Discount/Premium	-38%

Jindal Steel and Power Valuation and Intrinsic Share Price = INR 378.04

ASIAN PAINTS VALUATION

The company has 50+ years of market leadership in India. They have a dealer network of 65,000+ and is a leader across all geographies except the Kashmir region in India. Asian Paints have deeply penetrated the Indian market down to the rural economy where they sell distemper paints, to the automobile sector where they currently have 20% of the total market. The major competitors are Kansai Nerolac and Berger paints in India. These companies, however, have not been able to establish a solid market presence and compete with Asian paints in the organised sector. The company is also focused on R&D and introduces 25 colour additions every year. They also have installed paint dispensing (NNG) machines with almost all retailers which saves them warehousing and encourage retailers to sell Asian Paint products. From here, we go ahead with Asian Paints Valuation and Intrinsic Value of its shares.

Read more here: Asian Paints Shares Fundamental Analysis
Methodology Used:
Discounted cash flow (DCF) is a valuation method used to estimate the value of an investment based on its expected future cash flows. DCF analysis attempts to figure out the value of an investment today, based on projections of how much money it will generate in the future. The following step by step procedure is followed.

1. Determining the Revenue Growth Rates
2. Forecasting the Financial Statements

3. Deriving the FCFF and FCFE
4. Calculating the Terminal Value
5. Calculating the Discount Rate
6. Discounting the Cashflows
7. Arriving at the Intrinsic Value of the Shares

Step 1: Determining the Revenue Growth Rates

We arrive at the below table by using the past and expected future performance of both the company and the economy. This along with adjustments to changes in the management expectations, extraordinary events and other macro factors give the revenue growth rates for Asian Paints Valuation.

Financial Year	Revenue Growth Rate
Year 1	5%
Year 2	-2%
Year 3	21%
Year 4	14%
Year 5	13%

Step 2: Forecasting the Financial Statements

The financial statements are forecasted for a period of 5 years using the annual report data of the company. The assumptions used for forecasting are tabulated below. The Excel model is completely editable and can be adjusted for specific changes which may happen over a period of time.

Assumptions Control Sheet	
Income Statement	
Average COGS as Percentage of Revenue	58.63%
Research and Development as Percentage of Revenue	0.00%
Sales, General and administrative as Percentage of Revenue	5.95%
Other operating expenses as Percentage of Revenue	18.79%
Other income (expense) as Percentage of Revenue	1.39%
Balance Sheet	
Short Term Debt as Percentage of Total Assets	3.66%
Long Term Debt as Percentage of Total Assets	0.37%
Cash and Cash Equivalents as Percentage of Revenue	2.90%
Short Term Equivalents as Percentage of Revenue	9.14%
Accounts Receivables as Percentage of Revenue	9.39%
Inventory as Percentage of Revenue	16.05%
Prepaid Expenses as Percentage of Revenue	0.11%
Other Current Assets as Percentage of Revenue	3.67%
Gross property, plant and equipment as Percentage of Revenue	27.69%
Intangible assets as Percentage of Revenue	1.29%
Other long-term assets as Percentage of Revenue	10.26%
Accounts payable as Percentage of Revenue	12.16%
Corporate Tax Rate	22.00%
Other current liabilities as Percentage of Revenue	7.72%
Retained Earnings as as Percentage of Net Income	51.21%
Accumulated other comprehensive income as Percentage of Revenue	28.27%
Cashflow Statement	
Other Working Capital as Percentage of Revenue	0.33%

Step 3: Deriving the FCFF and FCFE

Free cash flow to the firm (FCFF) represents the amount of cash flow from operations available for distribution after accounting for depreciation expenses, taxes, working capital, and investments. FCFF is a measurement of a company's profitability after all expenses and reinvestments. It is given as follows.

Free cash flow to equity (FCFE) is a measure of how much cash is available to the equity shareholders of a company after all expenses, reinvestment, and debt are paid. FCFE is a measure of equity capital usage.

F/S Items (INR Millions)	Mar-20	Mar-21	Mar-22	Mar-23	Mar-24
Free Cash Flow	18406	16729	22853	28674	35398

to Firm					
Free Cash Flow to Equity	18825	17071	23776	29611	36458

Step 4: Calculating the Terminal Value

Terminal value (TV) is the value of a business or project beyond the forecast period when future cash flows can be estimated. It assumes that a business will grow at a set growth rate forever after the forecast period. Terminal value often comprises a large percentage of the total assessed value.

Terminal Value Calculation	Units INR Millions
Free Cash Flow to Firm	35397.67
Growth Rate	5.00%
Cost of Capital	8.54%
Terminal Value	1226740.34

Step 5: Calculating the Discount Rate

DCF analysis helps assess the viability of a project or investment by calculating the present value of expected future cash flows using a discount rate. Here we use the Weighted average cost of capital (WACC) to discount the cash flow. The below table from the excel model shows the calculation of WACC for Asian Paints Valuation.

Cost of Equity Calcuation using CAPM	
Risk Free Rate (5 year G-Sec)	5.18%
Stock Beta (Ref: Reuters)	0.41
Beta Unlevered B/(1+ D(1-t)/E)	0.39
Beta Relevered B*(1+ D(1-t)/E)	0.41
Market Return Rm (Nifty 50 10 Year CAGR)	14.25%
Cost of Equity	**8.88%**

Cost of Debt	
Cost of Debt (Interest Expense/Total Debt)	3.01%

Cost of Capital	
Cost of Equity	8.88%
Weight of Equity in Target Capital Structure	94.24%
Cost of Debt	3.01%
Weight of Debt in Capital Structure	5.76%
WACC	**8.54%**

Step 6: Discounting the Cashflows

The WACC and the Cost of Equity for the company calculated in the above step are then used to discount the FCFF, FCFE and Terminal Value calculated in Step 3 and 4. In our case, we'll only consider the FCFF based Intrinsic price of the shares as it represents the cash flow to all the suppliers of capital and not only to the equity shareholders. Thus we arrive at Present value of future FCFF for Asian Paints Valuation. (Units are INR Millions)

FCFF Calculation	FV	Discounted
Mar-20	18406.15	16957.28
Mar-21	16728.89	14198.87
Mar-22	22853.17	17870.08
Mar-23	28674.13	20656.83
Mar-24	35397.67	23493.16
Terminal Value	1226740.34	814177.97
Present Value (PV)		907354.19

FCFE Calculation	FV	Discounted
Mar-20	18824.68	17288.95
Mar-21	17071.32	14399.55
Mar-22	23776.49	18419.19
Mar-23	29611.32	21067.92
Mar-24	36458.04	23823.09
Terminal Value	1226740.34	801599.51
Present Value (PV)		896598.20

Step 7: Arriving at the Intrinsic Value of the Shares

Dividing the PV of the FCFF and Terminal Value (the Value of the entire firm) by the number of outstanding shares we get the per share intrinsic value. We can compare this price with the current market price of the stock to get the Discount or Premium to its intrinsic price.

Asian Paints Valuation	Units
PV in INR Million	907354
No of Shares Outstanding (In Million)	959
Intrinsic Value	946.15

BILLION DOLLAR VALUATION

Current Market Price of Share	2290.00
Current Discount/Premium	142%

Asian Paints Valuation and Intrinsic Share Price = INR 946.15

BIOCON VALUATION

The company operates in the pharmaceutical industry where market dominance is achieved through R&D, Regulatory Approvals, Scale, distribution and Branding. Biocon Biologics has a product pipeline of 28 molecules, including 11 partnered with Mylan, several with Sandoz and many being developed independently. The partnerships are such that the company aims to be an early mover in oncology, diabetes and Autoimmune Biosimilar drugs in the next 3-5 years. The company has approvals from EMA, US FDA, Health Canada, ANVISA, COFEPRIS, PMDA, TGA and MCC for manufacturing of biosimilars and their sale in 120+ countries in the world. From here, we go ahead with Biocon Valuation and Intrinsic Value of its shares.

Read more here: **Biocon Shares Fundamental Analysis**

Methodology Used:

Discounted cash flow (DCF) is a valuation method used to estimate the value of an investment based on its expected future cash flows. DCF analysis attempts to figure out the value of an investment today, based on projections of how much money it will generate in the future. The following step by step procedure is followed.

1. Determining the Revenue Growth Rates
2. Forecasting the Financial Statements
3. Deriving the FCFF and FCFE
4. Calculating the Terminal Value
5. Calculating the Discount Rate
6. Discounting the Cashflows

7. Arriving at the Intrinsic Value of the Shares

Step 1: Determining the Revenue Growth Rates

We arrive at the below table by using the past and expected future performance of both the company and the economy. This along with adjustments to changes in the management expectations, extraordinary events and other macro factors give the revenue growth rates for Biocon Valuation.

Financial Year	Revenue Growth Rate
Year 1	15%
Year 2	22%
Year 3	27%
Year 4	17%
Year 5	15%

Step 2: Forecasting the Financial Statements

The financial statements are forecasted for a period of 5 years using the annual report data of the company. The assumptions used for forecasting are tabulated below. The Excel model is completely editable and can be adjusted for specific changes which may happen over a period of time.

Assumptions Control Sheet	
Income Statement	
Average COGS as Percentage of Revenue	37.69%
Research and Development as Percentage of Revenue	6.50%
Sales, General and administrative as Percentage of Revenue	5.86%
Other operating expenses as Percentage of Revenue	38.49%
Other income (expense) as Percentage of Revenue	9.75%
Balance Sheet	
Short Term Debt as Percentage of Total Assets	4.97%
Long Term Debt as Percentage of Total Assets	0.00%
Cash and Cash Equivalents as Percentage of Revenue	15.28%
Short Term Equivalents as Percentage of Revenue	32.33%
Accounts Receivables as Percentage of Revenue	23.22%
Inventory as Percentage of Revenue	17.07%
Prepaid Expenses as Percentage of Revenue	1.76%
Other Current Assets as Percentage of Revenue	7.83%
Gross property, plant and equipment as Percentage of Revenue	152.27%
Intangible assets as Percentage of Revenue	10.71%
Other long-term assets as Percentage of Revenue	14.43%
Accounts payable as Percentage of Revenue	19.86%
Corporate Tax Rate	22.00%
Other current liabilities as Percentage of Revenue	16.39%
Retained Earnings as as Percentage of Net Income	108.20%
Accumulated other comprehensive income as Percentage of Revenue	14.53%
Cashflow Statement	
Other Working Capital as Percentage of Revenue	1.26%

Step 3: Deriving the FCFF and FCFE

Free cash flow to the firm (FCFF) represents the amount of cash flow from operations available for distribution after accounting for depreciation expenses, taxes, working capital, and investments. FCFF is a measurement of a company's profitability after all expenses and reinvestments. It is given as follows.

Free cash flow to equity (FCFE) is a measure of how much cash is available to the equity shareholders of a company after all expenses, reinvestment, and debt are paid. FCFE is a measure of equity capital usage.

F/S Items (INR Millions)	Mar-20	Mar-21	Mar-22	Mar-23	Mar-24
Free Cash Flow	6567	11425	18958	19691	23287

to Firm					
Free Cash Flow to Equity	16908	20576	38170	26632	27566

Step 4: Calculating the Terminal Value

Terminal value (TV) is the value of a business or project beyond the forecast period when future cash flows can be estimated. It assumes that a business will grow at a set growth rate forever after the forecast period. Terminal value often comprises a large percentage of the total assessed value.

Terminal Value Calculation	Units INR Millions
Free Cash Flow to Firm	23286.97
Growth Rate	5.00%
Cost of Capital	8.25%
Terminal Value	752299.96

Step 5: Calculating the Discount Rate

DCF analysis helps assess the viability of a project or investment by calculating the present value of expected future cash flows using a discount rate. Here we use the Weighted average cost of capital (WACC) to discount the cash flow. The below table from the excel model shows the calculation of WACC for Biocon Valuation.

Cost of Equity Calcuation using CAPM	
Risk Free Rate (5 year G-Sec)	5.18%
Stock Beta (Ref: Reuters)	0.56
Beta Unlevered B/(1+ D(1-t)/E)	0.50
Beta Relevered B*(1+ D(1-t)/E)	0.65
Market Return Rm (Nifty 50 10 Year CAGR)	14.25%
Cost of Equity	**11.09%**

Cost of Debt	
Cost of Debt (Interest Expense/Total Debt)	0.75%

Cost of Capital	
Cost of Equity	11.09%
Weight of Equity in Target Capital Structure	72.52%
Cost of Debt	0.75%
Weight of Debt in Capital Structure	27.48%
WACC	**8.25%**

Step 6: Discounting the Cashflows

The WACC and the Cost of Equity for the company calculated in the above step are then used to discount the FCFF, FCFE and Terminal Value calculated in Step 3 and 4. In our case, we'll only consider the FCFF based Intrinsic price of the shares as it represents the cash flow to all the suppliers of capital and not only to the equity shareholders. Thus we arrive at Present value of future FCFF for Biocon Valuation. (Units are INR Millions)

FCFF Calculation	FV	Discounted
Mar-20	6567.08	6066.58
Mar-21	11425.39	9750.20
Mar-22	18957.70	14945.12
Mar-23	19690.81	14339.98
Mar-24	23286.97	15666.40
Terminal Value	752299.96	506112.82
Present Value (PV)		566881.11

FCFE Calculation	FV	Discounted
Mar-20	16908.14	15219.69
Mar-21	20576.44	16672.09
Mar-22	38169.72	27838.68
Mar-23	26631.85	17484.00
Mar-24	27565.86	16289.99
Terminal Value	752299.96	444570.24
Present Value (PV)		538074.69

Step 7: Arriving at the Intrinsic Value of the Shares

Dividing the PV of the FCFF and Terminal Value (the Value of the entire firm) by the number of outstanding shares we get the per share intrinsic value. We can compare this price with the current market price of the stock to get the Discount or Premium to its intrinsic price.

Biocon Valuation	Units
PV in INR Million	566881
No of Shares Outstanding (In Million)	1183
Intrinsic Value	479.19

STOCK VALUATION HANDBOOK PART 2

Current Market Price of Share	432.00
Current Discount/Premium	-10%

Biocon Valuation and Intrinsic Share Price = INR 479.19

ACC CEMENTS VALUATION

ACC Cement currently has 17 manufacturing facilities and 75 ready to mix concrete plants in India. It sells approximately 30 million tonnes of cement in a year and has 10,000+ dealers in the Indian Subcontinent. Increase in the Government expenditure on infrastructure and road development projects are likely to be a major thrust for business growth to ACC. The company has seen a consistent increase in the volume of cement and RMX (Ready to Mix) cement since 2014. It has a large distributor network across India and has a market presence of about 80+ years in the Indian market. However, the cement business does not have a highly distinguished product or fat profit margins. The cement manufacturing process is such that the cost of electricity and transport comes to around 35% of the total cost. From here, we go ahead with ACC Cements Valuation and Intrinsic Value of its shares.

Read more here: ACC Cements Shares Fundamental Analysis
Methodology Used:
Discounted cash flow (DCF) is a valuation method used to estimate the value of an investment based on its expected future cash flows. DCF analysis attempts to figure out the value of an investment today, based on projections of how much money it will generate in the future. The following step by step procedure is followed.

1. Determining the Revenue Growth Rates
2. Forecasting the Financial Statements

3. Deriving the FCFF and FCFE
4. Calculating the Terminal Value
5. Calculating the Discount Rate
6. Discounting the Cashflows
7. Arriving at the Intrinsic Value of the Shares

Step 1: Determining the Revenue Growth Rates

We arrive at the below table by using the past and expected future performance of both the company and the economy. This along with adjustments to changes in the management expectations, extraordinary events and other macro factors give the revenue growth rates for ACC Cements Valuation.

Financial Year	Revenue Growth Rate
Year 1	-11%
Year 2	16%
Year 3	9%
Year 4	10%
Year 5	9%

Step 2: Forecasting the Financial Statements

The financial statements are forecasted for a period of 5 years using the annual report data of the company. The assumptions used for forecasting are tabulated below. The Excel model is completely editable and can be adjusted for specific changes which may happen over a period of time.

Assumptions Control Sheet	
Income Statement	
Average COGS as Percentage of Revenue	23.76%
Research and Development as Percentage of Revenue	0.00%
Sales, General and administrative as Percentage of Revenue	27.59%
Other operating expenses as Percentage of Revenue	38.96%
Other income (expense) as Percentage of Revenue	0.92%
Balance Sheet	
Short Term Debt as Percentage of Total Assets	3.00%
Long Term Debt as Percentage of Total Assets	5.00%
Cash and Cash Equivalents as Percentage of Revenue	20.18%
Short Term Equivalents as Percentage of Revenue	0.73%
Accounts Receivables as Percentage of Revenue	4.86%
Inventory as Percentage of Revenue	10.17%
Prepaid Expenses as Percentage of Revenue	2.63%
Other Current Assets as Percentage of Revenue	3.31%
Gross property, plant and equipment as Percentage of Revenue	67.24%
Intangible assets as Percentage of Revenue	0.28%
Other long-term assets as Percentage of Revenue	13.46%
Accounts payable as Percentage of Revenue	11.25%
Corporate Tax Rate	22.00%
Other current liabilities as Percentage of Revenue	19.31%
Retained Earnings as as Percentage of Net Income	73.41%
Accumulated other comprehensive income as Percentage of Revenue	21.34%
Cashflow Statement	
Other Working Capital as Percentage of Revenue	0.10%

Step 3: Deriving the FCFF and FCFE

Free cash flow to the firm (FCFF) represents the amount of cash flow from operations available for distribution after accounting for depreciation expenses, taxes, working capital, and investments. FCFF is a measurement of a company's profitability after all expenses and reinvestments. It is given as follows.

Free cash flow to equity (FCFE) is a measure of how much cash is available to the equity shareholders of a company after all expenses, reinvestment, and debt are paid. FCFE is a measure of equity capital usage.

F/S Items (INR Millions)	Mar-20	Mar-21	Mar-22	Mar-23	Mar-24
Free Cash Flow	11584	14184	15092	17021	18812

to Firm					
Free Cash Flow to Equity	26015	14757	15464	17504	19257

Step 4: Calculating the Terminal Value

Terminal value (TV) is the value of a business or project beyond the forecast period when future cash flows can be estimated. It assumes that a business will grow at a set growth rate forever after the forecast period. Terminal value often comprises a large percentage of the total assessed value.

Terminal Value Calculation	Units INR Millions
Free Cash Flow to Firm	18811.99
Growth Rate	5.00%
Cost of Capital	13.62%
Terminal Value	229036.56

Step 5: Calculating the Discount Rate

DCF analysis helps assess the viability of a project or investment by calculating the present value of expected future cash flows using a discount rate. Here we use the Weighted average cost of capital (WACC) to discount the cash flow. The below table from the excel model shows the calculation of WACC for ACC Cements Valuation.

Cost of Equity Calcuation using CAPM	
Risk Free Rate (5 year G-Sec)	5.18%
Stock Beta (Ref: Reuters)	0.95
Beta Unlevered B/(1+ D(1-t)/E)	0.95
Beta Relevered B*(1+ D(1-t)/E)	1.04
Market Return Rm (Nifty 50 10 Year CAGR)	14.25%
Cost of Equity	**14.65%**

Cost of Debt	
Cost of Debt (Interest Expense/Total Debt)	5.54%

Cost of Capital	
Cost of Equity	14.65%
Weight of Equity in Target Capital Structure	88.78%
Cost of Debt	5.54%
Weight of Debt in Capital Structure	11.22%
WACC	**13.62%**

Step 6: Discounting the Cashflows

The WACC and the Cost of Equity for the company calculated in the above step are then used to discount the FCFF, FCFE and Terminal Value calculated in Step 3 and 4. In our case, we'll only consider the FCFF based Intrinsic price of the shares as it represents the cash flow to all the suppliers of capital and not only to the equity shareholders. Thus we arrive at Present value of future FCFF for ACC Cements Valuation. (Units are INR Millions)

FCFF Calculation	FV	Discounted
Mar-20	11583.93	10194.95
Mar-21	14184.10	10986.51
Mar-22	15091.92	10288.02
Mar-23	17020.59	10211.54
Mar-24	18811.99	9933.00
Terminal Value	229036.56	120934.56
Present Value (PV)		172548.58

FCFE Calculation	FV	Discounted
Mar-20	26015.04	22691.59
Mar-21	14757.34	11227.65
Mar-22	15463.56	10261.96
Mar-23	17504.15	10132.17
Mar-24	19257.31	9722.94
Terminal Value	229036.56	115639.62
Present Value (PV)		179675.93

Step 7: Arriving at the Intrinsic Value of the Shares

Dividing the PV of the FCFF and Terminal Value (the Value of the entire firm) by the number of outstanding shares we get the per share intrinsic value. We can compare this price with the current market price of the stock to get the Discount or Premium to its intrinsic price.

ACC Cements Valuation	Units
PV in INR Million	172549
No of Shares Outstanding (In Million)	188
Intrinsic Value	917.81

BILLION DOLLAR VALUATION

Current Market Price of Share	1724.00
Current Discount/Premium	88%

ACC Cements Valuation and Intrinsic Share Price = INR 917.81

BRITANNIA VALUATION

Britannia Industries was established in 1892 by a group of British businessmen with an initial investment of INR 295. It is one of India's oldest existing companies and now a part of the Wadia Group headed by Nusli Wadia. Britannia is one of the most trusted food company in India and operates some well know brands like Good Day, Tiger, NutriChoice, Milk Bikis and Marie Gold. The company was also recently included in the Nifty-50 benchmark index. From here, we go ahead with Britannia Valuation and Intrinsic Value of its shares.

Read more here: Britannia Shares Fundamental Analysis
Methodology Used:
Discounted cash flow (DCF) is a valuation method used to estimate the value of an investment based on its expected future cash flows. DCF analysis attempts to figure out the value of an investment today, based on projections of how much money it will generate in the future. The following step by step procedure is followed.

1. Determining the Revenue Growth Rates
2. Forecasting the Financial Statements
3. Deriving the FCFF and FCFE
4. Calculating the Terminal Value
5. Calculating the Discount Rate
6. Discounting the Cashflows
7. Arriving at the Intrinsic Value of the Shares

Step 1: Determining the Revenue Growth Rates

We arrive at the below table by using the past and expected future performance of both the company and the economy. This along with adjustments to changes in the management expectations, extraordinary events and other macro factors give the revenue growth rates for Britannia Valuation.

Financial Year	Revenue Growth Rate
Year 1	4%
Year 2	15%
Year 3	10%
Year 4	11%
Year 5	10%

Step 2: Forecasting the Financial Statements

The financial statements are forecasted for a period of 5 years using the annual report data of the company. The assumptions used for forecasting are tabulated below. The Excel model is completely editable and can be adjusted for specific changes which may happen over a period of time.

Assumptions Control Sheet	
Income Statement	
Average COGS as Percentage of Revenue	61.24%
Research and Development as Percentage of Revenue	0.00%
Sales, General and administrative as Percentage of Revenue	10.38%
Other operating expenses as Percentage of Revenue	15.46%
Other income (expense) as Percentage of Revenue	1.86%
Balance Sheet	
Short Term Debt as Percentage of Total Assets	2.52%
Long Term Debt as Percentage of Total Assets	1.13%
Cash and Cash Equivalents as Percentage of Revenue	1.22%
Short Term Equivalents as Percentage of Revenue	6.09%
Accounts Receivables as Percentage of Revenue	2.58%
Inventory as Percentage of Revenue	6.41%
Prepaid Expenses as Percentage of Revenue	9.51%
Other Current Assets as Percentage of Revenue	1.27%
Gross property, plant and equipment as Percentage of Revenue	14.91%
Intangible assets as Percentage of Revenue	0.12%
Other long-term assets as Percentage of Revenue	6.23%
Accounts payable as Percentage of Revenue	9.47%
Corporate Tax Rate	22.00%
Other current liabilities as Percentage of Revenue	4.35%
Retained Earnings as as Percentage of Net Income	59.10%
Accumulated other comprehensive income as Percentage of Revenue	5.85%
Cashflow Statement	
Other Working Capital as Percentage of Revenue	-0.47%

Step 3: Deriving the FCFF and FCFE

Free cash flow to the firm (FCFF) represents the amount of cash flow from operations available for distribution after accounting for depreciation expenses, taxes, working capital, and investments. FCFF is a measurement of a company's profitability after all expenses and reinvestments. It is given as follows.

Free cash flow to equity (FCFE) is a measure of how much cash is available to the equity shareholders of a company after all expenses, reinvestment, and debt are paid. FCFE is a measure of equity capital usage.

F/S Items (INR Millions)	Mar-20	Mar-21	Mar-22	Mar-23	Mar-24
Free Cash Flow	10901	12797	14669	16654	19102

to Firm					
Free Cash Flow to Equity	11890	13110	14980	17014	19494

Step 4: Calculating the Terminal Value

Terminal value (TV) is the value of a business or project beyond the forecast period when future cash flows can be estimated. It assumes that a business will grow at a set growth rate forever after the forecast period. Terminal value often comprises a large percentage of the total assessed value.

Terminal Value Calculation	Units INR Millions
Free Cash Flow to Firm	19101.65
Growth Rate	6.00%
Cost of Capital	10.57%
Terminal Value	442836.19

Step 5: Calculating the Discount Rate

DCF analysis helps assess the viability of a project or investment by calculating the present value of expected future cash flows using a discount rate. Here we use the Weighted average cost of capital (WACC) to discount the cash flow. The below table from the excel model shows the calculation of WACC for Britannia Valuation.

Cost of Equity Calcuation using CAPM	
Risk Free Rate (5 year G-Sec)	5.18%
Stock Beta (Ref: Reuters)	0.62
Beta Unlevered B/(1+ D(1-t)/E)	0.60
Beta Relevered B*(1+ D(1-t)/E)	0.63
Market Return Rm (Nifty 50 10 Year CAGR)	14.25%
Cost of Equity	**10.86%**

Cost of Debt	
Cost of Debt (Interest Expense/Total Debt)	4.86%

Cost of Capital	
Cost of Equity	10.86%
Weight of Equity in Target Capital Structure	95.17%
Cost of Debt	4.86%
Weight of Debt in Capital Structure	4.83%
WACC	**10.57%**

Step 6: Discounting the Cashflows

The WACC and the Cost of Equity for the company calculated in the above step are then used to discount the FCFF, FCFE and Terminal Value calculated in Step 3 and 4. In our case, we'll only consider the FCFF based Intrinsic price of the shares as it represents the cash flow to all the suppliers of capital and not only to the equity shareholders. Thus we arrive at Present value of future FCFF for Britannia Valuation. (Units are INR Millions)

FCFF Calculation	FV	Discounted
Mar-20	10900.53	9858.28
Mar-21	12797.36	10467.13
Mar-22	14668.54	10850.45
Mar-23	16653.75	11141.07
Mar-24	19101.65	11556.85
Terminal Value	442836.19	267923.99
Present Value (PV)		321797.78

FCFE Calculation	FV	Discounted
Mar-20	11890.19	10725.17
Mar-21	13109.72	10666.56
Mar-22	14980.38	10994.34
Mar-23	17014.09	11263.43
Mar-24	19493.87	11640.60
Terminal Value	442836.19	264435.98
Present Value (PV)		319726.08

Step 7: Arriving at the Intrinsic Value of the Shares

Dividing the PV of the FCFF and Terminal Value (the Value of the entire firm) by the number of outstanding shares we get the per share intrinsic value. We can compare this price with the current market price of the stock to get the Discount or Premium to its intrinsic price.

Britannia Valuation	Units
PV in INR Million	321798
No of Shares Outstanding (In Million)	240
Intrinsic Value	1340.82

STOCK VALUATION HANDBOOK PART 2

Current Market Price of Share	3584.00
Current Discount/Premium	167%

Britannia Valuation and Intrinsic Share Price = INR 1340.82

CUMMINS VALUATION

Cummins has 5+ decades of presence in the Indian market and a manufacturing capacity of over 75,000+ engines per annum. The company powers 8 out of every 10 excavators, 9 out of 10 rail engines, 4 out of 10 gensets and each and every water rig in the Indian market. Cummins is also one of the largest exporters of engineering products in India. The company also invests heavily in R&D for design improvements and process efficiencies. From here, we go ahead with Cummins Valuation and Intrinsic Value of its shares.

Read more here: **Cummins Shares Fundamental Analysis**
Methodology Used:
Discounted cash flow (DCF) is a valuation method used to estimate the value of an investment based on its expected future cash flows. DCF analysis attempts to figure out the value of an investment today, based on projections of how much money it will generate in the future. The following step by step procedure is followed.

1. Determining the Revenue Growth Rates
2. Forecasting the Financial Statements
3. Deriving the FCFF and FCFE
4. Calculating the Terminal Value
5. Calculating the Discount Rate
6. Discounting the Cashflows
7. Arriving at the Intrinsic Value of the Shares

Step 1: Determining the Revenue Growth Rates
We arrive at the below table by using the past and expected fu-

ture performance of both the company and the economy. This along with adjustments to changes in the management expectations, extraordinary events and other macro factors give the revenue growth rates for Cummins Valuation.

Financial Year	Revenue Growth Rate
Year 1	-9%
Year 2	-15%
Year 3	16%
Year 4	12%
Year 5	13%

Step 2: Forecasting the Financial Statements

The financial statements are forecasted for a period of 5 years using the annual report data of the company. The assumptions used for forecasting are tabulated below. The Excel model is completely editable and can be adjusted for specific changes which may happen over a period of time.

Assumptions Control Sheet	
Income Statement	
Average COGS as Percentage of Revenue	66.74%
Research and Development as Percentage of Revenue	0.00%
Sales, General and administrative as Percentage of Revenue	1.95%
Other operating expenses as Percentage of Revenue	17.32%
Other Income (expense) as Percentage of Revenue	3.56%
Balance Sheet	
Short Term Debt as Percentage of Total Assets	3.94%
Long Term Debt as Percentage of Total Assets	0.00%
Cash and Cash Equivalents as Percentage of Revenue	2.56%
Short Term Equivalents as Percentage of Revenue	11.90%
Accounts Receivables as Percentage of Revenue	21.63%
Inventory as Percentage of Revenue	12.02%
Prepaid Expenses as Percentage of Revenue	1.24%
Other Current Assets as Percentage of Revenue	6.24%
Gross property, plant and equipment as Percentage of Revenue	44.81%
Intangible assets as Percentage of Revenue	#DIV/0!
Other long-term assets as Percentage of Revenue	17.43%
Accounts payable as Percentage of Revenue	13.25%
Corporate Tax Rate	22.00%
Other current liabilities as Percentage of Revenue	6.58%
Retained Earnings as as Percentage of Net Income	21.88%
Accumulated other comprehensive income as Percentage of Revenue	22.71%
Cashflow Statement	
Other Working Capital as Percentage of Revenue	1.03%

Step 3: Deriving the FCFF and FCFE

Free cash flow to the firm (FCFF) represents the amount of cash flow from operations available for distribution after accounting for depreciation expenses, taxes, working capital, and investments. FCFF is a measurement of a company's profitability after all expenses and reinvestments. It is given as follows.

Free cash flow to equity (FCFE) is a measure of how much cash is available to the equity shareholders of a company after all expenses, reinvestment, and debt are paid. FCFE is a measure of equity capital usage.

F/S Items (INR Millions)	Mar-20	Mar-21	Mar-22	Mar-23	Mar-24
Free Cash Flow to Firm	3744	3460	6859	7407	8602

| Free Cash Flow to Equity | 2954 | 3385 | 6934 | 7481 | 8696 |

Step 4: Calculating the Terminal Value

Terminal value (TV) is the value of a business or project beyond the forecast period when future cash flows can be estimated. It assumes that a business will grow at a set growth rate forever after the forecast period. Terminal value often comprises a large percentage of the total assessed value.

Terminal Value Calculation	Units INR Millions
Free Cash Flow to Firm	8602.19
Growth Rate	5.00%
Cost of Capital	12.19%
Terminal Value	135589.68

Step 5: Calculating the Discount Rate

DCF analysis helps assess the viability of a project or investment by calculating the present value of expected future cash flows using a discount rate. Here we use the Weighted average cost of capital (WACC) to discount the cash flow. The below table from the excel model shows the calculation of WACC for Cummins Valuation.

Cost of Equity Calcuation using CAPM	
Risk Free Rate (5 year G-Sec)	5.18%
Stock Beta (Ref: Reuters)	0.84
Beta Unlevered B/(1+ D(1-t)/E)	0.79
Beta Relevered B*(1+ D(1-t)/E)	0.83
Market Return Rm (Nifty 50 10 Year CAGR)	14.25%
Cost of Equity	**12.70%**

Cost of Debt	
Cost of Debt (Interest Expense/Total Debt)	**3.00%**

Cost of Capital	
Cost of Equity	12.70%
Weight of Equity in Target Capital Structure	94.82%
Cost of Debt	3.00%
Weight of Debt in Capital Structure	5.18%
WACC	**12.19%**

Step 6: Discounting the Cashflows

The WACC and the Cost of Equity for the company calculated in the above step are then used to discount the FCFF, FCFE and Terminal Value calculated in Step 3 and 4. In our case, we'll only consider the FCFF based Intrinsic price of the shares as it represents the cash flow to all the suppliers of capital and not only to the equity shareholders. Thus we arrive at Present value of future FCFF for Cummins Valuation. (Units are INR Millions)

FCFF Calculation	FV	Discounted
Mar-20	3744.06	3337.15
Mar-21	3460.34	2749.07
Mar-22	6858.90	4856.85
Mar-23	7407.15	4675.03
Mar-24	8602.19	4839.23
Terminal Value	135589.68	76277.02
Present Value (PV)		96734.35

FCFE Calculation	FV	Discounted
Mar-20	2954.29	2621.47
Mar-21	3384.57	2664.94
Mar-22	6933.65	4844.38
Mar-23	7480.80	4637.85
Mar-24	8695.51	4783.61
Terminal Value	135589.68	74591.16
Present Value (PV)		94143.42

Step 7: Arriving at the Intrinsic Value of the Shares

Dividing the PV of the FCFF and Terminal Value (the Value of the entire firm) by the number of outstanding shares we get the per share intrinsic value. We can compare this price with the current market price of the stock to get the Discount or Premium to its intrinsic price.

Cummins Valuation	Units
PV in INR Million	96734
No of Shares Outstanding (In Million)	277
Intrinsic Value	349.22

BILLION DOLLAR VALUATION

Current Market Price of Share	572.00
Current Discount/Premium	64%

Cummins Valuation and Intrinsic Share Price = INR 349.22

DCF Valuation

AVANTI FEEDS VALUATION

Avanti Feeds is the leading manufacturer of Prawn and Fish Feeds and Shrimp Processor and Exporter from India. The company has established a joint venture with Thai Union Frozen Products PCL., the world's largest seafood processors and leading manufacturer of prawn and fish feeds in Thailand with integrated facilities from Hatchery to Shrimp & Fish processing and Exports. From here, we go ahead with Avanti Feeds Valuation and Intrinsic Value of its shares.

Read more here: Avanti Feeds Shares Fundamental Analysis

Methodology Used:

Discounted cash flow (DCF) is a valuation method used to estimate the value of an investment based on its expected future cash flows. DCF analysis attempts to figure out the value of an investment today, based on projections of how much money it will generate in the future. The following step by step procedure is followed.

1. Determining the Revenue Growth Rates
2. Forecasting the Financial Statements
3. Deriving the FCFF and FCFE
4. Calculating the Terminal Value
5. Calculating the Discount Rate
6. Discounting the Cashflows
7. Arriving at the Intrinsic Value of the Shares

Step 1: Determining the Revenue Growth Rates
We arrive at the below table by using the past and expected future performance of both the company and the economy. This along with adjustments to changes in the management expectations, extraordinary events and other macro factors give the revenue growth rates for Avanti Feeds Valuation.

Financial Year	Revenue Growth Rate
Year 1	20%
Year 2	2%
Year 3	14%
Year 4	13%
Year 5	13%

Step 2: Forecasting the Financial Statements
The financial statements are forecasted for a period of 5 years using the annual report data of the company. The assumptions used for forecasting are tabulated below. The Excel model is completely editable and can be adjusted for specific changes which may happen over a period of time.

Assumptions Control Sheet	
Income Statement	
Average COGS as Percentage of Revenue	79.60%
Research and Development as Percentage of Revenue	0.00%
Sales, General and administrative as Percentage of Revenue	3.06%
Other operating expenses as Percentage of Revenue	4.03%
Other income (expense) as Percentage of Revenue	1.12%
Balance Sheet	
Short Term Debt as Percentage of Total Assets	1.57%
Long Term Debt as Percentage of Total Assets	0.39%
Cash and Cash Equivalents as Percentage of Revenue	1.37%
Short Term Equivalents as Percentage of Revenue	12.29%
Accounts Receivables as Percentage of Revenue	1.45%
Inventory as Percentage of Revenue	13.47%
Prepaid Expenses as Percentage of Revenue	0.21%
Other Current Assets as Percentage of Revenue	0.71%
Gross property, plant and equipment as Percentage of Revenue	9.73%
Intangible assets as Percentage of Revenue	0.01%
Other long-term assets as Percentage of Revenue	2.53%
Accounts payable as Percentage of Revenue	7.25%
Corporate Tax Rate	22.00%
Other current liabilities as Percentage of Revenue	1.31%
Retained Earnings as as Percentage of Net Income	56.47%
Accumulated other comprehensive income as Percentage of Revenue	10.60%
Cashflow Statement	
Other Working Capital as Percentage of Revenue	0.81%

Step 3: Deriving the FCFF and FCFE

Free cash flow to the firm (FCFF) represents the amount of cash flow from operations available for distribution after accounting for depreciation expenses, taxes, working capital, and investments. FCFF is a measurement of a company's profitability after all expenses and reinvestments. It is given as follows.

Free cash flow to equity (FCFE) is a measure of how much cash is available to the equity shareholders of a company after all expenses, reinvestment, and debt are paid. FCFE is a measure of equity capital usage.

F/S Items (INR Millions)	Mar-20	Mar-21	Mar-22	Mar-23	Mar-24
Free Cash Flow to Firm	3797	3947	3915	4882	6004

| Free Cash Flow to Equity | 4113 | 3984 | 3970 | 4944 | 6078 |

Step 4: Calculating the Terminal Value

Terminal value (TV) is the value of a business or project beyond the forecast period when future cash flows can be estimated. It assumes that a business will grow at a set growth rate forever after the forecast period. Terminal value often comprises a large percentage of the total assessed value.

Terminal Value Calculation	Units INR Millions
Free Cash Flow to Firm	6004.15
Growth Rate	6.00%
Cost of Capital	20.12%
Terminal Value	45059.29

Step 5: Calculating the Discount Rate

DCF analysis helps assess the viability of a project or investment by calculating the present value of expected future cash flows using a discount rate. Here we use the Weighted average cost of capital (WACC) to discount the cash flow. The below table from the excel model shows the calculation of WACC for Avanti Feeds Valuation.

Cost of Equity Calcuation using CAPM	
Risk Free Rate (5 year G-Sec)	5.18%
Stock Beta (Ref: Reuters)	1.67
Beta Unlevered B/(1+ D(1-t)/E)	1.66
Beta Relevered B*(1+ D(1-t)/E)	1.69
Market Return Rm (Nifty 50 10 Year CAGR)	14.25%
Cost of Equity	**20.55%**

Cost of Debt	
Cost of Debt (Interest Expense/Total Debt)	4.20%

Cost of Capital	
Cost of Equity	20.55%
Weight of Equity in Target Capital Structure	97.41%
Cost of Debt	4.20%
Weight of Debt in Capital Structure	2.59%
WACC	**20.12%**

Step 6: Discounting the Cashflows

The WACC and the Cost of Equity for the company calculated in the above step are then used to discount the FCFF, FCFE and Terminal Value calculated in Step 3 and 4. In our case, we'll only consider the FCFF based Intrinsic price of the shares as it represents the cash flow to all the suppliers of capital and not only to the equity shareholders. Thus we arrive at Present value of future FCFF for Avanti Feeds Valuation. (Units are INR Millions)

FCFF Calculation	FV	Discounted
Mar-20	3796.50	3160.48
Mar-21	3947.17	2735.41
Mar-22	3914.69	2258.41
Mar-23	4881.64	2344.44
Mar-24	6004.15	2400.45
Terminal Value	45059.29	18014.67
Present Value (PV)		30913.87

FCFE Calculation	FV	Discounted
Mar-20	4112.79	3411.77
Mar-21	3984.20	2741.75
Mar-22	3970.00	2266.31
Mar-23	4943.61	2341.09
Mar-24	6077.60	2387.53
Terminal Value	45059.29	17701.12
Present Value (PV)		30849.56

Step 7: Arriving at the Intrinsic Value of the Shares

Dividing the PV of the FCFF and Terminal Value (the Value of the entire firm) by the number of outstanding shares we get the per share intrinsic value. We can compare this price with the current market price of the stock to get the Discount or Premium to its intrinsic price.

Avanti Feeds Valuation	Units
PV in INR Million	30914
No of Shares Outstanding (In Million)	136
Intrinsic Value	227.31

Current Market Price of Share	548.00
Current Discount/Premium	141%

Avanti Feeds Valuation and Intrinsic Share Price = INR 227.31

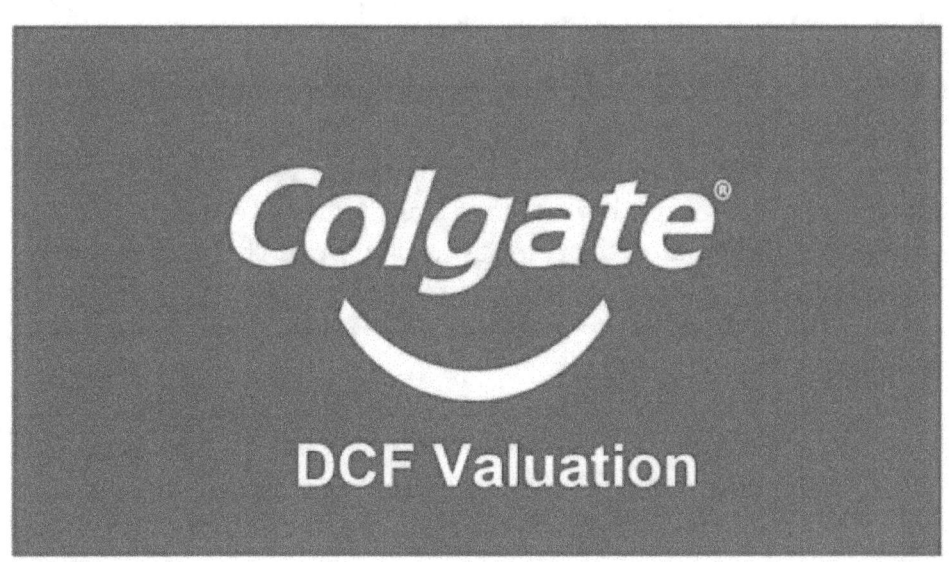

COLGATE PALMOLIVE VALUATION

Colgate currently has 88% of household penetration in India and reaches 241 million homes. It leads in 5 out of 8 categories of toothpaste and 4 out of 5 toothbrush category. Colgate has a robust distribution channel, especially in rural India. It currently faces competition from companies like Patanjali and Dabur, but its long presence of about 80+ years in India has fetched them good brand loyalty. From here, we go ahead with Colgate Palmolive Valuation and Intrinsic Value of its shares.

Read more here: **Colgate Palmolive Shares Fundamental Analysis**
Methodology Used:
Discounted cash flow (DCF) is a valuation method used to estimate the value of an investment based on its expected future cash flows. DCF analysis attempts to figure out the value of an investment today, based on projections of how much money it will generate in the future. The following step by step procedure is followed.

1. Determining the Revenue Growth Rates
2. Forecasting the Financial Statements
3. Deriving the FCFF and FCFE
4. Calculating the Terminal Value
5. Calculating the Discount Rate
6. Discounting the Cashflows
7. Arriving at the Intrinsic Value of the Shares

Step 1: Determining the Revenue Growth Rates

We arrive at the below table by using the past and expected future performance of both the company and the economy. This along with adjustments to changes in the management expectations, extraordinary events and other macro factors give the revenue growth rates for Colgate Palmolive Valuation.

Financial Year	Revenue Growth Rate
Year 1	3%
Year 2	5%
Year 3	8%
Year 4	10%
Year 5	12%

Step 2: Forecasting the Financial Statements

The financial statements are forecasted for a period of 5 years using the annual report data of the company. The assumptions used for forecasting are tabulated below. The Excel model is completely editable and can be adjusted for specific changes which may happen over a period of time.

Assumptions Control Sheet	
Income Statement	
Average COGS as Percentage of Revenue	42.23%
Research and Development as Percentage of Revenue	0.00%
Sales, General and administrative as Percentage of Revenue	13.63%
Other operating expenses as Percentage of Revenue	22.46%
Other income (expense) as Percentage of Revenue	0.77%
Balance Sheet	
Short Term Debt as Percentage of Total Assets	0.24%
Long Term Debt as Percentage of Total Assets	0.00%
Cash and Cash Equivalents as Percentage of Revenue	5.90%
Short Term Equivalents as Percentage of Revenue	0.18%
Accounts Receivables as Percentage of Revenue	3.48%
Inventory as Percentage of Revenue	6.41%
Prepaid Expenses as Percentage of Revenue	2.22%
Other Current Assets as Percentage of Revenue	3.42%
Gross property, plant and equipment as Percentage of Revenue	37.62%
Intangible assets as Percentage of Revenue	0.00%
Other long-term assets as Percentage of Revenue	4.22%
Accounts payable as Percentage of Revenue	14.16%
Corporate Tax Rate	22.00%
Other current liabilities as Percentage of Revenue	7.56%
Retained Earnings as as Percentage of Net Income	-9.76%
Accumulated other comprehensive income as Percentage of Revenue	9.66%
Cashflow Statement	
Other Working Capital as Percentage of Revenue	-0.66%

Step 3: Deriving the FCFF and FCFE

Free cash flow to the firm (FCFF) represents the amount of cash flow from operations available for distribution after accounting for depreciation expenses, taxes, working capital, and investments. FCFF is a measurement of a company's profitability after all expenses and reinvestments. It is given as follows.

Free cash flow to equity (FCFE) is a measure of how much cash is available to the equity shareholders of a company after all expenses, reinvestment, and debt are paid. FCFE is a measure of equity capital usage.

F/S Items (INR Millions)	Mar-20	Mar-21	Mar-22	Mar-23	Mar-24
Free Cash Flow to Firm	12729	10062	10253	10848	11757

| Free Cash Flow to Equity | 12732 | 10064 | 10256 | 10853 | 11763 |

Step 4: Calculating the Terminal Value

Terminal value (TV) is the value of a business or project beyond the forecast period when future cash flows can be estimated. It assumes that a business will grow at a set growth rate forever after the forecast period. Terminal value often comprises a large percentage of the total assessed value.

Terminal Value Calculation	Units INR Millions
Free Cash Flow to Firm	11756.52
Growth Rate	6.00%
Cost of Capital	9.68%
Terminal Value	338961.62

Step 5: Calculating the Discount Rate

DCF analysis helps assess the viability of a project or investment by calculating the present value of expected future cash flows using a discount rate. Here we use the Weighted average cost of capital (WACC) to discount the cash flow. The below table from the excel model shows the calculation of WACC for Colgate Palmolive Valuation.

Cost of Equity Calcuation using CAPM	
Risk Free Rate (5 year G-Sec)	5.18%
Stock Beta (Ref: Reuters)	0.50
Beta Unlevered B/(1+ D(1-t)/E)	0.50
Beta Relevered B*(1+ D(1-t)/E)	0.50
Market Return Rm (Nifty 50 10 Year CAGR)	14.25%
Cost of Equity	**9.73%**

Cost of Debt	
Cost of Debt (Interest Expense/Total Debt)	**3.00%**

Cost of Capital	
Cost of Equity	9.73%
Weight of Equity in Target Capital Structure	99.20%
Cost of Debt	3.00%
Weight of Debt in Capital Structure	0.80%
WACC	**9.68%**

Step 6: Discounting the Cashflows

The WACC and the Cost of Equity for the company calculated in the above step are then used to discount the FCFF, FCFE and Terminal Value calculated in Step 3 and 4. In our case, we'll only consider the FCFF based Intrinsic price of the shares as it represents the cash flow to all the suppliers of capital and not only to the equity shareholders. Thus we arrive at Present value of future FCFF for Colgate Palmolive Valuation. (Units are INR Millions)

FCFF Calculation	FV	Discounted
Mar-20	12729.33	11606.25
Mar-21	10062.36	8365.13
Mar-22	10252.89	7771.52
Mar-23	10848.08	7497.19
Mar-24	11756.52	7408.17
Terminal Value	338961.62	213590.87
Present Value (PV)		256239.12

FCFE Calculation	FV	Discounted
Mar-20	12732.06	11603.06
Mar-21	10063.83	8358.17
Mar-22	10256.23	7762.63
Mar-23	10852.97	7485.90
Mar-24	11763.32	7394.33
Terminal Value	338961.62	213068.58
Present Value (PV)		255672.66

Step 7: Arriving at the Intrinsic Value of the Shares

Dividing the PV of the FCFF and Terminal Value (the Value of the entire firm) by the number of outstanding shares we get the per share intrinsic value. We can compare this price with the current market price of the stock to get the Discount or Premium to its intrinsic price.

Colgate Palmolive Valuation	Units
PV in INR Million	256239
No of Shares Outstanding (In Million)	272
Intrinsic Value	942.06

Current Market Price of Share	1625.00
Current Discount/Premium	72%

Colgate Palmolive Valuation and Intrinsic Share Price = INR 942.06

BOSCH VALUATION

In India, Bosch is a leading supplier of technology and services in the areas of Mobility Solutions, Industrial Technology, Consumer Goods, and Energy and Building Technology. Additionally, Bosch has, in India, the largest development center outside Germany, for an end to end engineering and technology solutions. The company has grown over the years to include 18 manufacturing sites and seven development and application center in India. From here, we go ahead with Bosch Valuation and Intrinsic Value of its shares.

Read more here: **Bosch Shares Fundamental Analysis**

Methodology Used:

Discounted cash flow (DCF) is a valuation method used to estimate the value of an investment based on its expected future cash flows. DCF analysis attempts to figure out the value of an investment today, based on projections of how much money it will generate in the future. The following step by step procedure is followed.

1. Determining the Revenue Growth Rates
2. Forecasting the Financial Statements
3. Deriving the FCFF and FCFE
4. Calculating the Terminal Value
5. Calculating the Discount Rate
6. Discounting the Cashflows
7. Arriving at the Intrinsic Value of the Shares

Step 1: Determining the Revenue Growth Rates

We arrive at the below table by using the past and expected future performance of both the company and the economy. This along with adjustments to changes in the management expectations, extraordinary events and other macro factors give the revenue growth rates for Bosch Valuation.

Financial Year	Revenue Growth Rate
Year 1	-22%
Year 2	-10%
Year 3	23%
Year 4	14%
Year 5	13%

Step 2: Forecasting the Financial Statements

The financial statements are forecasted for a period of 5 years using the annual report data of the company. The assumptions used for forecasting are tabulated below. The Excel model is completely editable and can be adjusted for specific changes which may happen over a period of time.

STOCK VALUATION HANDBOOK PART 2

Assumptions Control Sheet	
Income Statement	
Average COGS as Percentage of Revenue	56.63%
Research and Development as Percentage of Revenue	0.00%
Sales, General and administrative as Percentage of Revenue	3.94%
Other operating expenses as Percentage of Revenue	26.41%
Other income (expense) as Percentage of Revenue	5.30%
Balance Sheet	
Short Term Debt as Percentage of Total Assets	0.20%
Long Term Debt as Percentage of Total Assets	0.28%
Cash and Cash Equivalents as Percentage of Revenue	1.75%
Short Term Equivalents as Percentage of Revenue	24.41%
Accounts Receivables as Percentage of Revenue	12.99%
Inventory as Percentage of Revenue	11.91%
Prepaid Expenses as Percentage of Revenue	0.00%
Other Current Assets as Percentage of Revenue	8.28%
Gross property, plant and equipment as Percentage of Revenue	21.57%
Intangible assets as Percentage of Revenue	0.00%
Other long-term assets as Percentage of Revenue	39.77%
Accounts payable as Percentage of Revenue	14.07%
Corporate Tax Rate	22.00%
Other current liabilities as Percentage of Revenue	11.46%
Retained Earnings as as Percentage of Net Income	76.21%
Accumulated other comprehensive income as Percentage of Revenue	29.95%
Cashflow Statement	
Other Working Capital as Percentage of Revenue	-1.59%

Step 3: Deriving the FCFF and FCFE

Free cash flow to the firm (FCFF) represents the amount of cash flow from operations available for distribution after accounting for depreciation expenses, taxes, working capital, and investments. FCFF is a measurement of a company's profitability after all expenses and reinvestments. It is given as follows.

Free cash flow to equity (FCFE) is a measure of how much cash is available to the equity shareholders of a company after all expenses, reinvestment, and debt are paid. FCFE is a measure of equity capital usage.

F/S Items (INR Millions)	Mar-20	Mar-21	Mar-22	Mar-23	Mar-24
Free Cash Flow to Firm	13322	8334	11692	12779	18115

| Free Cash Flow to Equity | 13902 | 8321 | 11729 | 12815 | 18158 |

Step 4: Calculating the Terminal Value

Terminal value (TV) is the value of a business or project beyond the forecast period when future cash flows can be estimated. It assumes that a business will grow at a set growth rate forever after the forecast period. Terminal value often comprises a large percentage of the total assessed value.

Terminal Value Calculation	Units INR Millions
Free Cash Flow to Firm	18114.90
Growth Rate	5.00%
Cost of Capital	19.14%
Terminal Value	134544.24

Step 5: Calculating the Discount Rate

DCF analysis helps assess the viability of a project or investment by calculating the present value of expected future cash flows using a discount rate. Here we use the Weighted average cost of capital (WACC) to discount the cash flow. The below table from the excel model shows the calculation of WACC for Bosch Valuation.

Cost of Equity Calcuation using CAPM	
Risk Free Rate (5 year G-Sec)	5.18%
Stock Beta (Ref: Reuters)	1.54
Beta Unlevered B/(1+ D(1-t)/E)	1.54
Beta Relevered B*(1+ D(1-t)/E)	1.55
Market Return Rm (Nifty 50 10 Year CAGR)	14.25%
Cost of Equity	**19.21%**

Cost of Debt	
Cost of Debt (Interest Expense/Total Debt)	6.50%

Cost of Capital	
Cost of Equity	19.21%
Weight of Equity in Target Capital Structure	99.39%
Cost of Debt	6.50%
Weight of Debt in Capital Structure	0.61%
WACC	**19.14%**

Step 6: Discounting the Cashflows

The WACC and the Cost of Equity for the company calculated in the above step are then used to discount the FCFF, FCFE and Terminal Value calculated in Step 3 and 4. In our case, we'll only consider the FCFF based Intrinsic price of the shares as it represents the cash flow to all the suppliers of capital and not only to the equity shareholders. Thus we arrive at Present value of future FCFF for Bosch Valuation. (Units are INR Millions)

FCFF Calculation	FV	Discounted
Mar-20	13321.90	11181.99
Mar-21	8334.07	5871.69
Mar-22	11692.43	6914.55
Mar-23	12778.90	6343.16
Mar-24	18114.90	7547.46
Terminal Value	134544.24	56057.03
Present Value (PV)		93915.88

FCFE Calculation	FV	Discounted
Mar-20	13902.26	11661.52
Mar-21	8321.47	5855.17
Mar-22	11729.47	6922.90
Mar-23	12814.80	6344.40
Mar-24	18157.90	7540.75
Terminal Value	134544.24	55874.54
Present Value (PV)		94199.28

Step 7: Arriving at the Intrinsic Value of the Shares

Dividing the PV of the FCFF and Terminal Value (the Value of the entire firm) by the number of outstanding shares we get the per share intrinsic value. We can compare this price with the current market price of the stock to get the Discount or Premium to its intrinsic price.

Bosch Valuation	Units
PV in INR Million	93916
No of Shares Outstanding (In Million)	30
Intrinsic Value	3130.53

Current Market Price of Share	13182.00
Current Discount/Premium	321%

Bosch Valuation and Intrinsic Share Price = INR 3130.53

DCF Valuation

ITC VALUATION

The company operates across many industries, but all of them requires scale and branding for achieving market dominance. ITC strives towards diversified portfolio offerings away from its traditional cigarette business. The company has more than a century of presence in the Indian market and is now a dominant player in Paper and Paperboards, Agri-Business, FMCG and Hotels. Some of the largest non-tobacco brands include Ashirvad with revenue of INR 4500+ Crores, Sunfeast with a revenue of INR 3800+ Crore, Bingo with a revenue of INR 2500+ crore and Classmate with a revenue of INR 1400+ crore. Each set of business has its competitors and different market conditions, but overall ITC has been successful in establishing its dominance in the Indian market because of its scale, brands and distribution network. From here, we go ahead with ITC Valuation and Intrinsic Value of its shares.

Read more here: ITC Shares Fundamental Analysis
ITC Shares Relative Valuation
Methodology Used:
Discounted cash flow (DCF) is a valuation method used to estimate the value of an investment based on its expected future cash flows. DCF analysis attempts to figure out the value of an investment today, based on projections of how much money it will generate in the future. The following step by step procedure is followed.

1. Determining the Revenue Growth Rates
2. Forecasting the Financial Statements
3. Deriving the FCFF and FCFE

4. Calculating the Terminal Value
5. Calculating the Discount Rate
6. Discounting the Cashflows
7. Arriving at the Intrinsic Value of the Shares

Step 1: Determining the Revenue Growth Rates

We arrive at the below table by using the past and expected future performance of both the company and the economy. This along with adjustments to changes in the management expectations, extraordinary events and other macro factors give the revenue growth rates for ITC Valuation.

Financial Year	Revenue Growth Rate
Year 1	4%
Year 2	-3%
Year 3	20%
Year 4	15%
Year 5	13%

Step 2: Forecasting the Financial Statements

The financial statements are forecasted for a period of 5 years using the annual report data of the company. The assumptions used for forecasting are tabulated below. The Excel model is completely editable and can be adjusted for specific changes which may happen over a period of time.

Assumptions Control Sheet	
Income Statement	
Average COGS as Percentage of Revenue	36.00%
Research and Development as Percentage of Revenue	0.11%
Sales, General and administrative as Percentage of Revenue	3.71%
Other operating expenses as Percentage of Revenue	24.00%
Other income (expense) as Percentage of Revenue	4.09%
Balance Sheet	
Short Term Debt as Percentage of Total Assets	0.11%
Long Term Debt as Percentage of Total Assets	0.00%
Cash and Cash Equivalents as Percentage of Revenue	0.59%
Short Term Equivalents as Percentage of Revenue	32.39%
Accounts Receivables as Percentage of Revenue	6.20%
Inventory as Percentage of Revenue	19.45%
Prepaid Expenses as Percentage of Revenue	2.46%
Other Current Assets as Percentage of Revenue	2.25%
Gross property, plant and equipment as Percentage of Revenue	50.96%
Intangible assets as Percentage of Revenue	1.15%
Other long-term assets as Percentage of Revenue	26.75%
Accounts payable as Percentage of Revenue	6.63%
Corporate Tax Rate	22.00%
Other current liabilities as Percentage of Revenue	11.41%
Retained Earnings as as Percentage of Net Income	40.48%
Accumulated other comprehensive income as Percentage of Revenue	47.51%
Cashflow Statement	
Other Working Capital as Percentage of Revenue	-0.67%

Step 3: Deriving the FCFF and FCFE

Free cash flow to the firm (FCFF) represents the amount of cash flow from operations available for distribution after accounting for depreciation expenses, taxes, working capital, and investments. FCFF is a measurement of a company's profitability after all expenses and reinvestments. It is given as follows.

Free cash flow to equity (FCFE) is a measure of how much cash is available to the equity shareholders of a company after all expenses, reinvestment, and debt are paid. FCFE is a measure of equity capital usage.

F/S Items (INR Millions)	Mar-20	Mar-21	Mar-22	Mar-23	Mar-24
Free Cash Flow to Firm	129781	117486	158711	191364	226849

STOCK VALUATION HANDBOOK PART 2

| Free Cash Flow to Equity | 130576 | 117520 | 158790 | 191454 | 226950 |

Step 4: Calculating the Terminal Value

Terminal value (TV) is the value of a business or project beyond the forecast period when future cash flows can be estimated. It assumes that a business will grow at a set growth rate forever after the forecast period. Terminal value often comprises a large percentage of the total assessed value.

Terminal Value Calculation	Units INR Millions
Free Cash Flow to Firm	226848.68
Growth Rate	6.00%
Cost of Capital	12.16%
Terminal Value	3904521.78

Step 5: Calculating the Discount Rate

DCF analysis helps assess the viability of a project or investment by calculating the present value of expected future cash flows using a discount rate. Here we use the Weighted average cost of capital (WACC) to discount the cash flow. The below table from the excel model shows the calculation of WACC for ITC Valuation.

Cost of Equity Calcuation using CAPM	
Risk Free Rate (5 year G-Sec)	5.18%
Stock Beta (Ref: Reuters)	0.77
Beta Unlevered B/(1+ D(1-t)/E)	0.77
Beta Relevered B*(1+ D(1-t)/E)	0.77
Market Return Rm (Nifty 50 10 Year CAGR)	14.25%
Cost of Equity	**12.17%**

Cost of Debt	
Cost of Debt (Interest Expense/Total Debt)	**3.06%**

Cost of Capital	
Cost of Equity	12.17%
Weight of Equity in Target Capital Structure	99.87%
Cost of Debt	3.06%
Weight of Debt in Capital Structure	0.13%
WACC	**12.16%**

Step 6: Discounting the Cashflows

The WACC and the Cost of Equity for the company calculated in the above step are then used to discount the FCFF, FCFE and Terminal Value calculated in Step 3 and 4. In our case, we'll only consider the FCFF based Intrinsic price of the shares as it represents the cash flow to all the suppliers of capital and not only to the equity shareholders. Thus we arrive at Present value of future FCFF for ITC Valuation. (Units are INR Millions)

FCFF Calculation	FV	Discounted
Mar-20	129780.72	115711.90
Mar-21	117486.33	93394.87
Mar-22	158710.63	112488.87
Mar-23	191364.15	120929.42
Mar-24	226848.68	127813.13
Terminal Value	3904521.78	2199920.93
Present Value (PV)		2770259.12

FCFE Calculation	FV	Discounted
Mar-20	130576.17	116408.47
Mar-21	117519.73	93401.12
Mar-22	158790.45	112508.76
Mar-23	191453.52	120933.32
Mar-24	226950.06	127800.79
Terminal Value	3904521.78	2198725.99
Present Value (PV)		2769778.46

Step 7: Arriving at the Intrinsic Value of the Shares

Dividing the PV of the FCFF and Terminal Value (the Value of the entire firm) by the number of outstanding shares we get the per share intrinsic value. We can compare this price with the current market price of the stock to get the Discount or Premium to its intrinsic price.

ITC Valuation	Units
PV in INR Million	2770259
No of Shares Outstanding (In Million)	12231
Intrinsic Value	226.49

Current Market Price of Share	214.75
Current Discount/Premium	-5%

ITC Valuation and Intrinsic Share Price = INR 226.49

MOTHERSON SUMI VALUATION

Motherson is one of the world's largest manufacturers of components for the automotive and transport industries. Motherson Sumi Systems was established in 1986 and is a part of the Motherson Group. It is a joint venture between Samvardhana Motherson International Ltd of India and Sumitomo Wiring Systems Ltd. (SWS) of Japan. From here, we go ahead with Motherson Sumi Valuation and Intrinsic Value of its shares.

Read more here: Motherson Sumi Shares Fundamental Analysis
Methodology Used:
Discounted cash flow (DCF) is a valuation method used to estimate the value of an investment based on its expected future cash flows. DCF analysis attempts to figure out the value of an investment today, based on projections of how much money it will generate in the future. The following step by step procedure is followed.

1. Determining the Revenue Growth Rates
2. Forecasting the Financial Statements
3. Deriving the FCFF and FCFE
4. Calculating the Terminal Value
5. Calculating the Discount Rate
6. Discounting the Cashflows
7. Arriving at the Intrinsic Value of the Shares

Step 1: Determining the Revenue Growth Rates
We arrive at the below table by using the past and expected future performance of both the company and the economy. This along with adjustments to changes in the management expectations, extraordinary events and other macro factors give the revenue growth rates for Motherson Sumi Valuation.

Financial Year	Revenue Growth Rate
Year 1	-1%
Year 2	-12%
Year 3	20%
Year 4	11%
Year 5	12%

Step 2: Forecasting the Financial Statements
The financial statements are forecasted for a period of 5 years using the annual report data of the company. The assumptions used for forecasting are tabulated below. The Excel model is completely editable and can be adjusted for specific changes which may happen over a period of time.

Assumptions Control Sheet	
Income Statement	
Average COGS as Percentage of Revenue	58.00%
Research and Development as Percentage of Revenue	0.00%
Sales, General and administrative as Percentage of Revenue	3.00%
Other operating expenses as Percentage of Revenue	28.00%
Other income (expense) as Percentage of Revenue	-0.07%
Balance Sheet	
Short Term Debt as Percentage of Total Assets	6.16%
Long Term Debt as Percentage of Total Assets	31.34%
Cash and Cash Equivalents as Percentage of Revenue	6.29%
Short Term Equivalents as Percentage of Revenue	0.63%
Accounts Receivables as Percentage of Revenue	10.64%
Inventory as Percentage of Revenue	6.86%
Prepaid Expenses as Percentage of Revenue	1.65%
Other Current Assets as Percentage of Revenue	5.22%
Gross property, plant and equipment as Percentage of Revenue	28.49%
Intangible assets as Percentage of Revenue	2.74%
Other long-term assets as Percentage of Revenue	4.36%
Accounts payable as Percentage of Revenue	15.73%
Corporate Tax Rate	22.00%
Other current liabilities as Percentage of Revenue	6.23%
Retained Earnings as as Percentage of Net Income	64.81%
Accumulated other comprehensive income as Percentage of Revenue	1.67%
Cashflow Statement	
Other Working Capital as Percentage of Revenue	-0.66%

Step 3: Deriving the FCFF and FCFE

Free cash flow to the firm (FCFF) represents the amount of cash flow from operations available for distribution after accounting for depreciation expenses, taxes, working capital, and investments. FCFF is a measurement of a company's profitability after all expenses and reinvestments. It is given as follows.

Free cash flow to equity (FCFE) is a measure of how much cash is available to the equity shareholders of a company after all expenses, reinvestment, and debt are paid. FCFE is a measure of equity capital usage.

F/S Items (INR Millions)	Mar-20	Mar-21	Mar-22	Mar-23	Mar-24
Free Cash Flow to Firm	34048	27441	38325	46013	55189

| Free Cash Flow to Equity | 210333 | 16916 | 54040 | 61496 | 65811 |

Step 4: Calculating the Terminal Value

Terminal value (TV) is the value of a business or project beyond the forecast period when future cash flows can be estimated. It assumes that a business will grow at a set growth rate forever after the forecast period. Terminal value often comprises a large percentage of the total assessed value.

Terminal Value Calculation	Units INR Millions
Free Cash Flow to Firm	55188.93
Growth Rate	5.00%
Cost of Capital	14.65%
Terminal Value	600692.28

Step 5: Calculating the Discount Rate

DCF analysis helps assess the viability of a project or investment by calculating the present value of expected future cash flows using a discount rate. Here we use the Weighted average cost of capital (WACC) to discount the cash flow. The below table from the excel model shows the calculation of WACC for Motherson Sumi Valuation.

Cost of Equity Calcuation using CAPM	
Risk Free Rate (5 year G-Sec)	5.18%
Stock Beta (Ref: Reuters)	1.23
Beta Unlevered B/(1+ D(1-t)/E)	0.99
Beta Relevered B*(1+ D(1-t)/E)	2.04
Market Return Rm (Nifty 50 10 Year CAGR)	14.25%
Cost of Equity	**23.65%**

Cost of Debt	
Cost of Debt (Interest Expense/Total Debt)	8.01%

Cost of Capital	
Cost of Equity	23.65%
Weight of Equity in Target Capital Structure	42.41%
Cost of Debt	8.01%
Weight of Debt in Capital Structure	57.59%
WACC	**14.65%**

Step 6: Discounting the Cashflows

The WACC and the Cost of Equity for the company calculated in the above step are then used to discount the FCFF, FCFE and Terminal Value calculated in Step 3 and 4. In our case, we'll only consider the FCFF based Intrinsic price of the shares as it represents the cash flow to all the suppliers of capital and not only to the equity shareholders. Thus we arrive at Present value of future FCFF for Motherson Sumi Valuation. (Units are INR Millions)

FCFF Calculation	FV	Discounted
Mar-20	34048.07	29698.19
Mar-21	27440.51	20876.96
Mar-22	38325.14	25432.93
Mar-23	46013.37	26633.87
Mar-24	55188.93	27863.76
Terminal Value	600692.28	303277.28
Present Value (PV)		433783.00

FCFE Calculation	FV	Discounted
Mar-20	210332.90	170098.63
Mar-21	16916.19	11063.43
Mar-22	54039.82	28582.14
Mar-23	61495.66	26303.83
Mar-24	65811.44	22765.09
Terminal Value	600692.28	207787.81
Present Value (PV)		466600.92

Step 7: Arriving at the Intrinsic Value of the Shares

Dividing the PV of the FCFF and Terminal Value (the Value of the entire firm) by the number of outstanding shares we get the per share intrinsic value. We can compare this price with the current market price of the stock to get the Discount or Premium to its intrinsic price.

Motherson Sumi Valuation	Units
PV in INR Million	433783
No of Shares Outstanding (In Million)	3158
Intrinsic Value	137.36

Current Market Price of Share	142
Current Discount/Premium	3.3%

Motherson Sumi Valuation and Intrinsic Share Price = INR 137.36

TRENT VALUATION

Trent is the retail hand of the Tata group and was started in 1998. Trent operates Westside, one of the fast-growing retail chains in India based in Mumbai and Landmark a bookstore chain with brick and mortar stores in various locations of India. The company is one of the leading players in the branded retail industry in India and competes with some of the well-known fashion brands from the Aditya Birla Group and Shoppers Stop.

Read more here: **Trent Shares Fundamental Analysis**

Methodology Used:

Discounted cash flow (DCF) is a valuation method used to estimate the value of an investment based on its expected future cash flows. DCF analysis attempts to figure out the value of an investment today, based on projections of how much money it will generate in the future. The following step by step procedure is followed.

1. Determining the Revenue Growth Rates
2. Forecasting the Financial Statements
3. Deriving the FCFF and FCFE
4. Calculating the Terminal Value
5. Calculating the Discount Rate
6. Discounting the Cashflows
7. Arriving at the Intrinsic Value of the Shares

Step 1: Determining the Revenue Growth Rates

We arrive at the below table by using the past and expected future performance of both the company and the economy. This along with adjustments to changes in the management expectations, extraordinary events and other macro factors give the revenue growth rates for Trent Valuation.

Financial Year	Revenue Growth Rate
Year 1	32%
Year 2	-30%
Year 3	70%
Year 4	30%
Year 5	35%

Step 2: Forecasting the Financial Statements

The financial statements are forecasted for a period of 5 years using the annual report data of the company. The assumptions used for forecasting are tabulated below. The Excel model is completely editable and can be adjusted for specific changes which may happen over a period of time.

Assumptions Control Sheet	
Income Statement	
Average COGS as Percentage of Revenue	50.00%
Research and Development as Percentage of Revenue	0.00%
Sales, General and administrative as Percentage of Revenue	6.50%
Other operating expenses as Percentage of Revenue	35.00%
Other income (expense) as Percentage of Revenue	11.00%
Balance Sheet	
Short Term Debt as Percentage of Total Assets	11.57%
Long Term Debt as Percentage of Total Assets	6.06%
Cash and Cash Equivalents as Percentage of Revenue	1.66%
Short Term Equivalents as Percentage of Revenue	2.79%
Accounts Receivables as Percentage of Revenue	0.64%
Inventory as Percentage of Revenue	17.45%
Prepaid Expenses as Percentage of Revenue	6.30%
Other Current Assets as Percentage of Revenue	2.89%
Gross property, plant and equipment as Percentage of Revenue	37.67%
Intangible assets as Percentage of Revenue	0.65%
Other long-term assets as Percentage of Revenue	56.23%
Accounts payable as Percentage of Revenue	9.74%
Corporate Tax Rate	22.00%
Other current liabilities as Percentage of Revenue	4.43%
Retained Earnings as as Percentage of Net Income	47.15%
Accumulated other comprehensive income as Percentage of Revenue	24.12%
Cashflow Statement	
Other Working Capital as Percentage of Revenue	0.15%

Step 3: Deriving the FCFF and FCFE

Free cash flow to the firm (FCFF) represents the amount of cash flow from operations available for distribution after accounting for depreciation expenses, taxes, working capital, and investments. FCFF is a measurement of a company's profitability after all expenses and reinvestments. It is given as follows.

Free cash flow to equity (FCFE) is a measure of how much cash is available to the equity shareholders of a company after all expenses, reinvestment, and debt are paid. FCFE is a measure of equity capital usage.

F/S Items (INR Millions)	Mar-20	Mar-21	Mar-22	Mar-23	Mar-24
Free Cash Flow to Firm	4722	2396	5366	7804	11433

| Free Cash Flow to Equity | 13796 | -6627 | 15075 | 14925 | 22945 |

Step 4: Calculating the Terminal Value

Terminal value (TV) is the value of a business or project beyond the forecast period when future cash flows can be estimated. It assumes that a business will grow at a set growth rate forever after the forecast period. Terminal value often comprises a large percentage of the total assessed value.

Terminal Value Calculation	Units INR Millions
Free Cash Flow to Firm	11433.42
Growth Rate	6.00%
Cost of Capital	8.99%
Terminal Value	405889.54

Step 5: Calculating the Discount Rate

DCF analysis helps assess the viability of a project or investment by calculating the present value of expected future cash flows using a discount rate. Here we use the Weighted average cost of capital (WACC) to discount the cash flow. The below table from the excel model shows the calculation of WACC for Trent Valuation.

Cost of Equity Calcuation using CAPM	
Risk Free Rate (5 year G-Sec)	5.18%
Stock Beta (Ref: Reuters)	0.82
Beta Unlevered B/(1+ D(1-t)/E)	0.66
Beta Relevered B*(1+ D(1-t)/E)	1.19
Market Return Rm (Nifty 50 10 Year CAGR)	14.25%
Cost of Equity	**16.00%**

Cost of Debt	
Cost of Debt (Interest Expense/Total Debt)	2.11%

Cost of Capital	
Cost of Equity	16.00%
Weight of Equity in Target Capital Structure	49.53%
Cost of Debt	2.11%
Weight of Debt in Capital Structure	50.47%
WACC	**8.99%**

Step 6: Discounting the Cashflows

The WACC and the Cost of Equity for the company calculated in the above step are then used to discount the FCFF, FCFE and Terminal Value calculated in Step 3 and 4. In our case, we'll only consider the FCFF based Intrinsic price of the shares as it represents the cash flow to all the suppliers of capital and not only to the equity shareholders. Thus we arrive at Present value of future FCFF for Trent Valuation. (Units are INR Millions)

FCFF Calculation	FV	Discounted
Mar-20	4722.06	4332.73
Mar-21	2396.08	2017.25
Mar-22	5366.42	4145.47
Mar-23	7803.60	5531.13
Mar-24	11433.42	7435.75
Terminal Value	405889.54	263971.14
Present Value (PV)		287433.47

FCFE Calculation	FV	Discounted
Mar-20	13795.68	11893.12
Mar-21	-6626.82	-4925.05
Mar-22	15075.12	9658.71
Mar-23	14925.29	8243.92
Mar-24	22945.29	10925.91
Terminal Value	405889.54	193273.25
Present Value (PV)		229069.86

Step 7: Arriving at the Intrinsic Value of the Shares

Dividing the PV of the FCFF and Terminal Value (the Value of the entire firm) by the number of outstanding shares we get the per share intrinsic value. We can compare this price with the current market price of the stock to get the Discount or Premium to its intrinsic price.

Trent Valuation	Units
PV in INR Million	287433
No of Shares Outstanding (In Million)	332
Intrinsic Value	865.76

Current Market Price of Share	690.00
Current Discount/Premium	-25%

Trent Valuation and Intrinsic Share Price = INR 865.76

End of Book 2

www.ingramcontent.com/pod-product-compliance
Lightning Source LLC
Chambersburg PA
CBHW050004230526
45465CB00003BB/1249